DISASTERS AND HEROIC RESCUES SERIES

DISASTERS AND HEROIC RESCUES OF CALIFORNIA

Ray Jones and Joe Lubow

INSIDERS' GUIDE®

GUILFORD, CONNECTICUT
AN IMPRINT OF THE GLOBE PEQUOT PRESS

To buy books in quantity for corporate use
or incentives, call **(800) 962–0973, ext. 4551,**
or e-mail **premiums@GlobePequot.com.**

INSIDERS' GUIDE®

Copyright © 2006 Morris Book Publishing, LLC.

All rights reserved. No part of this book may be reproduced or transmitted in any form by any means, electronic or mechanical, including photocopying and recording, or by any information storage and retrieval system, except as may be expressly permitted by the 1976 Copyright Act or by the publisher. Requests for permission should be made in writing to The Globe Pequot Press, P.O. Box 480, Guilford, Connecticut 06437.

Insiders' Guide and TwoDot are registered trademarks of Morris Book Publishing, LLC.

Cover photo of Kearney Street after the 1906 San Francisco earthquake and fire is courtesy of the Library of Congress, LC-DIG-ppmsca-09832

A portion of Chapter 2 was originally published in *Lost Lighthouses* by Tim Harrison and Ray Jones; reprinted with permission.

Text design by Bill Brown Design
Map by M. A. Dubé © Morris Book Publishing, LLC.

Library of Congress Cataloging-in-Publication Data
Jones, Ray, 1948–
  Disasters and heroic rescues of California/Ray Jones and Joe Lubow.
    p. cm.—(Disasters and heroic rescues series)
  Includes bibliographical references.
  ISBN 0-7627-3822-7
    1. Natural disasters—California—History. 2. Disasters—California—History. 3. Rescues—California—History. 4. California—History. I. Lubow, Joseph M. II. Title. III. Series.
  GB5010.J66 2006
  979.4—dc22
                                                              2005024326

Manufactured in the United States of America
First Edition/First Printing

Acknowledgments

Our sincerest thanks to Globe Pequot Press Executive Editor Laura Strom for giving us a chance to tell these fascinating and often heart-rending California disaster stories. Thanks also to our editor, Amy Paradysz, for her insights, helpful advice, and—above all—patience. We deeply appreciate the rather amazing research assistance provided by Peter Blossom, who was able to find photographs where we thought none existed. And a special thanks to Allen Spiegel, who introduced the two rather lonely wordsmiths (Joe and Ray) and so made possible this collaboration. We are better writers and better people for knowing one another.

    I would also like to thank Rebecca Bergeon of the Interlibrary Loan department, Dennis Sun in circulation and other staff and librarians of California State University at Monterey Bay Library, as well as the librarians at Central Branch of the Santa Cruz Public Library, whose help was invaluable in researching this book. Also, thanks to my sister, Marsha Lubow, Michael Wreszin, and David Steinberg, and to my loving partner, Dr. Tran Ngoc Angie.

—*Joe Lubow*

I would like to express my appreciation to all my friends at Globe Pequot and elsewhere—at least I hope they are still my friends—who put up with me during this last very overworked year. And finally, thanks to all the thousands of Californians and others who came to the aid of the many disaster victims mentioned in this book and of all those struck by the inevitable calamities of the future.

—*Ray Jones*

Contents

Introduction
— ix —

CHAPTER 1
Lost in the Frozen Sierra
DONNER PARTY (1846–1847)
— 1 —

CHAPTER 2
Ship-Killing Rocks
WRECKS OFF POINT HONDA (1854 AND 1923)
— 11 —

CHAPTER 3
The Colorado Changes Course
MAKING OF THE SALTON SEA (1905)
— 17 —

CHAPTER 4
Terror in San Francisco
EARTHQUAKE AND FIRE (1906)
— 35 —

CHAPTER 5
Crime of the Century
LOS ANGELES TIMES BOMBING (1910)
— 51 —

CHAPTER 6
Fire in the Hole
ARGONAUT MINE DISASTER (1922)
– 69 –

CHAPTER 7
Mulholland's Dam Falls
ST. FRANCIS RESERVOIR FLOOD (1928)
– 81 –

CHAPTER 8
Friendly Fire
PORT CHICAGO EXPLOSION (1944)
– 89 –

CHAPTER 9
Trapped by Flame
RATTLESNAKE FOREST FIRE (1953)
– 97 –

CHAPTER 10
Rains That Wouldn't Stop
SANTA CRUZ CHRISTMAS FLOOD (1955)
– 103 –

CHAPTER 11
Wall of Water
CRESCENT CITY TSUNAMI (1964)
– 109 –

CHAPTER 12
He Shot the Pilot
CRASHES OF PAL 773 AND PSA 1771 (1964 AND 1987)
— 117 —

CHAPTER 13
The Longest Minute
SYLMAR EARTHQUAKE (1971)
— 123 —

CHAPTER 14
We've Been Hit
MAJOR AIRLINE COLLISIONS (1971, 1978, AND 1986)
— 127 —

CHAPTER 15
World Series Earthquake
LOMA PRIETA (1989)
— 135 —

CHAPTER 16
Poisoning the Sacramento
DUNSMUIR TOXIC SPILL (1991)
— 147 —

CHAPTER 17
Burning Hills
OAKLAND TUNNEL FIRE (1991)
— 153 —

CHAPTER 18

Shakedown in Los Angeles

NORTHRIDGE EARTHQUAKE (1994)

– 159 –

CHAPTER 19

For the Loss of a Screw

CRASH OF ALASKA AIRLINES 261 (2000)

– 165 –

Bibliography

– 173 –

About the Authors

– 187 –

Introduction

It is an extravagant vision that many follow to this day. They pack up their belongings, bid farewell to family and friends, and set out for California. People have been doing this since at least the 1840s when the first wagon trains left Missouri and headed toward the setting sun across an ocean of sage. Those early California-bound adventurers endured hardships that are impossible for us to imagine, and many of them died along the trail. So why did they do it? Why did they drive their oxen, their wagons, their families, and themselves across 2,500 miles of hostile wilderness? Probably if they had known what they would endure, they would never have left home.

Even today people are willing to risk a lot in order move to California. They give up decent paying jobs, comfortable homes, lifelong relationships, and much more in exchange for—well, they are not entirely certain. The only thing they know for sure is that they want to go. California is their dream.

It's true. California is every bit as much a dream as it is a place, and Americans have long clung to it as an article of faith. Most of us are still believers. There is more sunshine in California, more pretty women, more handsome men, more delicious food, more tasty wine, more opportunity—more of everything. And it's all there for the taking.

The problem is that on the road to California the dream is nearly always bumpier than we had expected, and California the place is never exactly as we imagine it should be. So we try to force the place to fit the dream, even if that means bending the laws of nature a bit, and this inevitably leads to something California definitely has more of than most states—disasters.

Disasters and Heroic Rescues of California recounts almost two dozen of California's most profound calamities. One—the notorious Donner Party incident—took place well before California became a state. Others, such as the 1994 Northridge earthquake in Los Angeles

County, are memories as recent as they are painful. But whether they happened during the days of the Gold Rush or only a few years ago, each of these disasters is linked, and not just because they occurred in or near California.

A pair of related themes runs through each of the stories you are about to read: the unrealistic expectations of some, if not all, Californians and a consistent unwillingness to show respect for the powerful, often deadly forces of nature. Both these factors—call them human failings, if you will—were present in George Donner and James Reed, who in 1846 led more than eighty once-hopeful pioneers straight into the teeth of the granddaddy of all California disasters. These factors were apparent in the famous 1906 earthquake and fire in San Francisco, a city built in an area known to be prone to massive temblors. People and houses were crammed together in early twentieth-century San Francisco, and inadequate precautions were taken against fires. The city was a disaster waiting to happen. So was Santa Cruz, where many homes and businesses built in a highly vulnerable floodplain were swept away in the great Christmas flood of 1955.

Earthquakes, floods, and other such cataclysms are not in and of themselves disasters. They are merely violent manifestations of natural processes endlessly repeated over hundreds of millions of years. The disaster lies in placing human beings and human structures squarely in the path of upheavals that are sooner or later bound to occur.

You may think that some of the calamities we describe—airline crashes, for instance—do not fit this pattern. But read the tragic stories of US Air West 706, PSA 182, and Aeromexico 498, all doomed by midair collisions—the result of overcrowded flyways—and you may change your mind.

Some of the characters in our tales of California calamity are clearly villains. It was the greed of William Mulholland and his cronies that led to construction of the St. Francis Dam, which collapsed, sending a man-made tsunami tumbling through the city.

Others, oddly enough, are half villain and half hero. James Reed's overzealous optimism and egregious misjudgments helped set the stage for the Donner Party tragedy, and he murdered a man. But it was also Reed who courageously led a relief expedition through the Sierra in the dead of winter to save more than half his companions from death by starvation and freezing.

However, most of our characters are neither villains nor heroes. They are merely victims—41 in the Donner Party in 1846–1847; 415 aboard the side-wheeler *Yankee Blade* in 1854; as many as 4,000 (450 officially) in the 1906 San Francisco earthquake and fire; 20 in the so-called Los Angeles Times bombing in 1910; 47 in the Argonaut mine fire in 1922; 23 in the wreck of seven U.S. Navy destroyers at Point Honda in 1923; more than 400 in the St. Francis Dam collapse in 1928; 320 in the Port Chicago explosions in 1944; 14 firefighters in the Rattlesnake fire at Mendocino in 1953; an entire city district in the Santa Cruz Christmas flood in 1955; 66 in the Sylmar earthquake near Los Angeles in 1971; 67 in the Loma Prieta "World Series" earthquake in 1989; 25 in the Oakland Hills fire also in 1991; 57 in the Northridge earthquake in 1994; and more than 600 in half a dozen major airliner crashes between 1958 and 1987.

There have been other California disasters, of course, and many other victims. There will be more. This book has nineteen chapters, and the twentieth is yet to be written.

CHAPTER 1

Lost in the Frozen Sierra

DONNER PARTY
- 1846–1847 -

OF ALL THE CALAMITIES THAT HAVE BEFALLEN California and Californians, none weighs more heavily on the human spirit than the one that struck a group of early westward-ho migrants in the high Sierra Nevada during the winter of 1846–1847. They are known to history as the Donner Party, and their grim fate has been recounted endlessly in bone-chilling tales told around campfires or on long winter drives through western mountain passes. It's a popular yarn because, as California disaster stories go, it has everything—

Donner Lake from summit. Originally published 1866. Library of Congress overzealous ambition, unrealistic expectations, poor judgment, bad timing, terrible luck, and a lack of due respect for the awesome power of nature. There are heroic acts of self-sacrifice and an equally heroic rescue of survivors. There is also the dark stain of murder and—as anyone who has ever heard of the incident knows—cannibalism.

Like most disasters this one began long before the events that are usually recounted. Its roots lay in the waves of migration that started moving westward in the early 1840s. It is hard to say what got the wheels of the first great wagon trains turning. Perhaps it was hard times and joblessness or the threat of cholera in the cities or the disappearance of cheap land in the East. More likely, however, it was a reawakening of a golden dream that had driven Americans westward since colonial times—the notion that, out there somewhere, a better life waited.

In the spring of 1846, that peculiarly American wanderlust burned in the hearts of George Donner and James Reed, who, along with more than twenty members of their two extended families, packed up their belongings, bid farewell to friends, and set out for California. Donner was a prosperous Illinois farmer and Reed a wealthy Springfield businessman, so these were not desperate people in need of a change of fortune. Their reasons for joining the thousands of other pioneers who set off into the wilderness that year were more personal than financial. Donner had already moved fives times before settling in Illinois, and now, at the age of sixty-two, he craved one more great adventure. Reed, whose restless intelligence had helped earn him a small fortune, hoped to prove himself anew in the West.

In the beginning the Donner Party numbered thirty-two, counting wives, children, various relatives, and half a dozen or so hired hands and teamsters to help drive the nine heavy wagons. Among the latter was the Reed's jumbo family wagon, a veritable house on wheels. The Reeds called it their "pioneer palace car." A two-story contraption equipped with bunks and a built-in iron stove, it broke the hearts of more than a few of the oxen that struggled to pull it. Despite the heft of their wagons, which other pioneers they met along the way considered extravagant, the party reached Independence, Missouri, without serious incident.

Most westward-bound migrants rested their animals at Independence and gathered themselves for the long push ahead. Between Independence and the Pacific lay three mighty mountain ranges, a series or scorching deserts, and more than 2,000 miles of wilderness. The crossing could be accomplished, as nearly half a million Americans would eventually prove, but it was not a journey to be undertaken lightly. For one thing it had to be completed in just six months, from the time, usually in May, when the mud on the high plains left behind by the spring rains began to dry out, until late autumn, when blizzards swept over the Sierra and blocked the passes with snow.

Leaving Independence on May 12, the Donners and Reeds were neither the first nor the last of the 1846 pioneers to crack their whips and launch themselves into the great western ocean of grass and sage. At first they made good progress, but inevitably, there were delays— broken wheels, tired animals, and sick children. It was frustrating, and as they rattled along through wagon ruts so deep that many remain to this day, they began to consider ways to make up for lost time.

Most wagons heading west that year, as in other years, followed a heavily beaten path that arched north of the Wasatch Mountains and the Great Salt Lake all the way to the foot of the Sierra. But George Donner had in his possession the so-called *Emigrant's Guide to Oregon and California,* in which the author, Lansford Hastings, recommended a shortcut. The new route plunged through the Wasatch Range rather than around it and crossed the utterly barren flats to the south of the Salt Lake. It would—Hastings claimed—lop several hundred miles off the trip. For days on end Donner and Reed discussed the shortcut option and, despite warnings from trappers and mountain men they met along the way, finally decided to chance it.

On July 18 the wagons rumbled across the Continental Divide, which nearly every westbound traveler considered the point of no return. Two days later they reached the Little Sandy River, where they parted ways with most of the other pioneers headed for California that year. Turning south toward Fort Bridger and away from the main trail, the nine Reed and Donner wagons were accompanied by twenty others owned by fellow migrants who likewise hoped to save time by taking the so-called Hastings Cut. The Donner Party of legend had formed.

Soon after they left the Little Sandy, the heads of the various families who had decided to take the shortcut met and — though businessman James Reed might have seemed a more logical choice — selected George Donner as their leader. Few thought Donner would lead for long anyway since they expected to meet up with Langsford Hastings at Fort Bridger just a few days up ahead. They had heard that Hastings was waiting there to show travelers the way through Hastings Cut.

What no one in the Donner Party realized, however, was that Hastings knew very little about the shortcut he had so glowingly described in his book. He had never explored it and was actually seeing it himself for the very first time that year. Hastings was what in our own time might be described as a "fast-talking promoter." Having visited California a few years earlier, he was determined to build an empire there and make himself its emperor. To that end, Hastings needed to get a lot people to California in a hurry, and he thought the shortcut just might serve his purpose. Instead, it proved a disaster for more than a few unwary travelers who wandered into it, the most unfortunate of these being the eighty-odd hapless members of the Donner Party.

By the time Donner, Reed, and the others reached Fort Bridger on July 31, Hastings had already left at the head of another small train of wagons. George Donner urged his charges on in an effort to catch up with Hastings but to no avail. Deeper and deeper they descended into the tangle of canyons and scrubby growth that lay before them, but try as they might, they could not catch up to Hastings. Meanwhile, precious time evaporated as the Donner Party crawled along, felling large trees, shoving aside boulders, and often covering little more than 2 miles in a day. And as they creaked and stumbled through the Wasatch and across the Great Basin, autumn, with its mountain blizzards, marched inexorably toward them.

The seemingly endless white salt flats beyond the shores of the Great Salt Lake nearly destroyed the party. Hastings had written that this 80-mile-wide desert could be crossed in "two days of hard driving." Instead, the crossing took five days, and by the time the pioneers reached the other side many of their precious oxen had either run off or died of thirst. Several wagons had to be abandoned, including the Reed family's cherished "pioneer palace."

As the last week of September approached, it became clear that the remaining supplies were insufficient to last the rest of the journey. Riders Charles Stanton and William McCutcheon were sent ahead to California to bring back help. Meanwhile the exhausted Donner Party pushed on, finally rejoining the main wagon trail near the Humboldt River on September 26. Hasting's "shortcut" had proven more than 100 miles longer than the old trail and cost them several weeks they could not afford to lose. Already some of the distant peaks were tinged with snow. Time was running out.

As they lunged for the Sierra hoping to get there ahead of the heavy snows, tempers frayed. A fight erupted when James Reed attempted to restrain a teamster named John Snyder who was beating oxen with the butt of a bullwhip. When it was over, Snyder lay dead with Reed's hunting knife buried in his chest. Reed was accused of murder, and some wanted to hang him. Instead, he was banished and forced to ride off into the wilds to a fate most thought little better than hanging. Ironically, this tragedy would end up saving half the members of the otherwise doomed Donner Party.

Misfortune continued to dog the little wagon train. A week after Snyder's death a Paiute Indian raiding party killed nearly two dozen oxen with poison arrows. Even so, the company managed to stagger on to the Truckee River and the foot of the Sierra, which they reached on October 16. Then, just three days later, the Donner Party's luck seemed to change when Charles Stanton returned from Sutter's Fort on the far side of the mountains with seven mules loaded with food and supplies. Spirits soared. Perhaps they would reach safety after all.

After several days of rest—desperately needed by all but especially by the remaining hard-pressed oxen—the Donner Party made its final push on the Sierra passes. With Stanton and a pair of Indian guides in the lead, it seemed for a while as if they would make it over. But then it began to snow, and snow. Just a few hundred feet from the summit, axle-deep drifts forced them to turn their wagons and head back down the mountain. The race was over. The mountain passes were blocked.

Pitching a rough camp beside Truckee Lake deep in the lofty Sierra, the Donner Party tried to settle in for the winter. What shelter they could build offered little protection from the cold, sleet, and snow. There were no medical supplies. What food they had soon ran out. By December most were attempting to sustain themselves with boiled leather, leaves, bones, and bark. Halfway through the month people began to die. The first was Balis Williams, one of the Reed's hired hands.

Few believed any of the party could survive the entire winter, and about a week before Christmas, a group of fifteen, ten men and five women, tried to walk out over the summit. They called themselves "the forlorn hope" after an expression used by soldiers when attacking a besieged fortress. The first troops chosen to scale the walls of the enemy were referred to as "The Forlorn Hope," and like them the fifteen pioneers fully expected to die. Even so, they were determined

These tree stumps, cut by the Donner Party, show how high the snow was. Library of Congress

to try. Anything was better than languishing beside the rock-hard frozen lake waiting to starve to death or freeze.

Using makeshift snowshoes, the forlorn hope trudged over the mountains for more than a week. At first in the lead, Charles Stanton was soon blinded by the snow. Eventually, he grew too sick and exhausted to continue and begged the others to leave him and push ahead. Reluctantly, they did.

Nine days out, the remaining members of the totally exhausted group finally lost all hope and stopped walking. Most had not eaten for days, and all knew they were dying. With snow and sleet pelting down through the darkness on Christmas Eve someone made a suggestion. They would hold a drawing to see who would be killed, cooked, and eaten so that the others might live. A man named Patrick Dolan drew the unlucky slip, but no one would agree to kill him. The next day he died anyway along with three other members of the party. All were butchered and eaten.

With the strength given them by this grisly sustenance, the remnants of the Forlorn Hope stumbled onward through the white mountains. Three more people were eaten, including a pair of mostly frozen Indian guides who were murdered for their flesh. Then on January 17, more than a month after they had left the Donner Party camp beside Truckee Lake, the seven remaining members of the company found a settler's cabin in the western foothills of the Sierra. All five women had survived the journey, but only two of the men had lived to tell their horrifying tale.

Back at Truckee Lake the dying continued. After a while the living stopped trying to chop through the ice to bury their dead companions. The frozen bodies were simply left on the bare ground and covered with blankets or heaps of snow. Most had given up hope and had stopped looking up toward the blinding white summit of the pass to watch for a rescue party. It seemed obvious to them that none was on the way. Actually, an attempt had been made to reach them way back in November. It was led by none other than James Reed.

Banished from the Donner wagon train for killing John Snyder, Reed had pressed on alone, reaching John Sutter's Fort on the far side of the Sierra in late October. The other pioneers who knew the Donner Party was still out on the trail had waited and watched, but no one had tried to put together a relief party. Desperate to save his wife Margaret and their five children, Reed quickly organized one. A few days out, Reed and his companion ran head on into a blizzard and had to turn back.

Even history now turned against the Donner Party. War had broken out between the United States and Mexico, and the fighting had spread to California. By the time Reed returned to Sutter's Fort to seek additional help in reaching his family and friends, every able-bodied man in the area had gone off to fight the Mexicans. With the passes now clogged by snow, Reed had no choice but to wait.

The waiting ended when the arrival of the battered and bleeding survivors of the forlorn hope on the west side of Sierra made it clear that those they had left behind at Truckee Lake would surely die without assistance—and soon. By early February two separate relief expeditions—one of them led by Reed—were pushing into the mountains. They did not reach the Truckee camp until the third week of the month. What they found there astonished and horrified them. Many had died, and some of those who still lived had begun to eat the dead.

To his immense relief Reed found among the living his beloved wife and children. What food the rescue parties could spare was distributed to the gaunt survivors. Then two dozen of them, including the Reed family, were evacuated over the mountains to safety.

Those left behind could only hope that additional rescue parties were on the way. Indeed several other expeditions were dispatched from Fort Sutter, the final one in late April. By the time the last mule train left Truckee Lake, forty-one members of the Donner Party had perished. Among the dead were George Donner, his wife Tamsen, and four of their children.

Forty-six members of the party survived to reach golden California and make what they could of the dreams it had held for them. As he had planned all along, James Reed went into business and earned a second fortune, buying and selling land. Settling south of the San Francisco Bay, he became a leading citizen of the town of San Jose.

Not surprisingly, few of the Donner Party survivors would talk openly of their experiences. One who did was Lewis Keseburg, but his admission to having eaten human flesh earned him no friends, and he soon fell silent on the subject. Keseburg struck it rich during the Gold Rush and later opened a successful restaurant in Sacramento.

A key player in the Donner Party tragedy who had not shared in the party's terrible suffering was Langsford Hastings. He practiced law briefly in San Francisco but was none too successful. Sympathetic to the South during the Civil War, Hastings wrote a new book, *The Emigrant's Guide to Brazil,* and tried to establish a refuge for Confederates in the Amazon. He died in 1870 never having admitted he had misled anyone by recommending a "shortcut" that turned out to be longer and harder than the original wagon train route. He rarely if ever spoke of the year 1846.

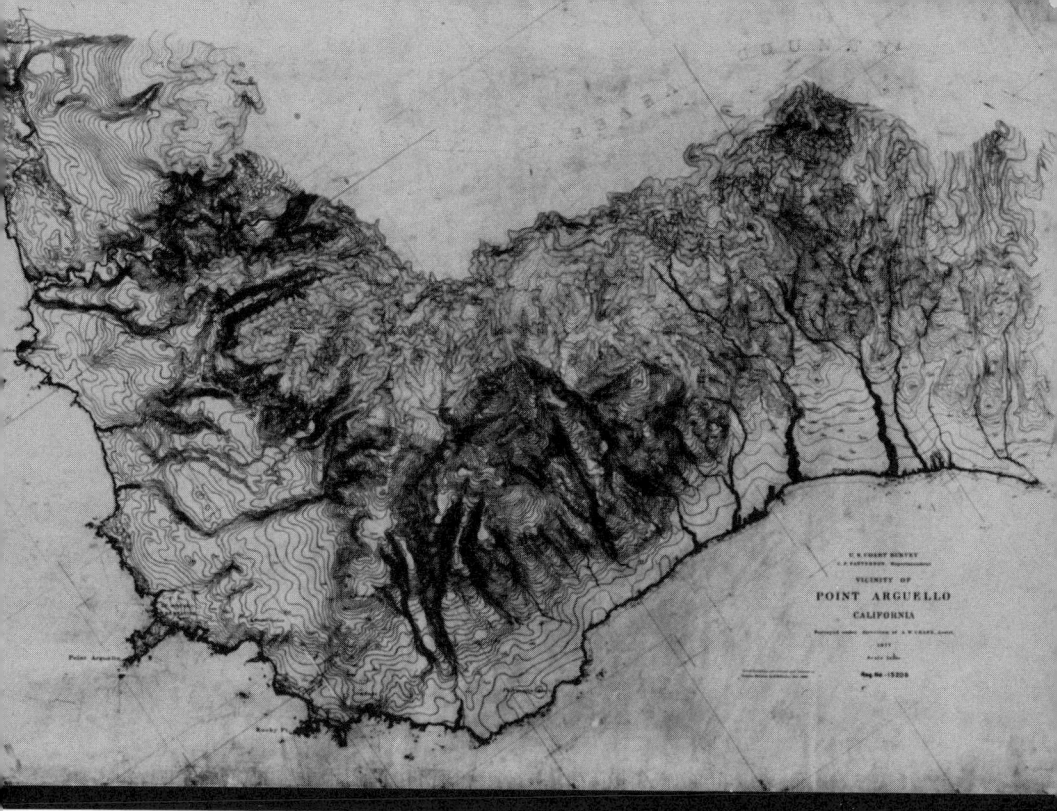

CHAPTER 2
Ship-Killing Rocks
WRECKS OFF POINT HONDA
- 1854 and 1923 -

ABOUT 300 MILES SOUTH OF SAN FRANCISCO, THE generally southward trending coast of California turns sharply toward the east, forming a jagged elbow that has been the ruin of many a fine ship and stout sailor. This seaward protrusion consists of a pair of rugged headlands known as Point Arguello and Point Conception. The latter marks the entrance to the Santa Barbara Channel, and navigators who steer toward the east just past Point Conception will sail

Confusing Point Conception and rocky Point Arguello is a dangerous mistake. The Yankee Blade *wrecked here during the Gold Rush era, followed by the* Delphy *in 1923.* National Oceanic & Atmospheric Administration (NOAA)

on in safe, mostly calm waters. Point Arguello, on the other hand, marks nothing but a 25-mile wall of solid rock reaching down toward Conception. As a result, mariners who confuse the two capes are likely doomed. More than a few vessels have been lost because their masters believed they had rounded Point Conception when, in fact, they were near Point Arguello.

Probably the worst such disaster took place in 1854 at a time when Gold Rush prospectors were still scouring the California hills in pursuit of yellow metal and sudden wealth. Indeed, many of the more than 400 victims of the wreck were thought to have carried fortunes in gold dust with them to the bottom of the Pacific, and the ship in question, the *Yankee Blade,* was heavily loaded, not just with passengers but with a ton or more of bullion.

Launched in 1853 in New York, the *Yankee Blade* was a 275-foot side-wheel steamer displacing 1,767 tons. Having served for a few months on the East Coast, she was purchased by Cornelius Vanderbilt and dispatched by way of Cape Horn to California. There she was expected to increase the tycoon's already sizeable fortune by providing reliable, steam-powered passenger service to those who could afford it—namely successful California businessmen and miners who had struck it rich in the goldfields.

On September 30, the *Yankee Blade* took on 822 passengers and a shipment of gold estimated to have been worth more than $150,000. Counting the captain and crew, there were nearly a thousand people on board when the ship set sail that same afternoon from San Francisco. Steaming out through the Golden Gate, the vessel turned south toward Panama, a destination she was not fated to reach.

With the weather favorable and her big engines churning—steam power was a very new thing in those days—the voyage went well for more than a day. Then, the *Yankee Blade*'s master made the same mistake another captain would make nearly seventy years later. He ordered his ship to turn eastward into the Santa Barbara Channel

The wreck of the Yankee Blade, *as she appeared on October 1, 1854.* Courtesy of The Bancroft Library, University of California, Berkeley

before actually having cleared Point Conception. By the time the error became apparent, it was already too late. The *Yankee Blade* struck rocks about 300 yards off Point Honda, and stuck fast.

Her hull fatally punctured, the *Yankee Blade* began to sink while her screaming passengers fought one another for places in lifeboats that proved too few in number to save all of them. Many fell or were pushed overboard and drowned. Ironically, more than a few had gold in their pockets, and the heavy metal dragged them to their deaths. Others discarded their gold before jumping overboard, hoping to swim ashore unencumbered. Most who attempted to swim through the pounding surf were crushed or swept out to sea.

Little more than half of those on board did eventually reach land, but even there they were not safe. Hearing of the wreck, merciless bandits descended on Point Honda, and many of the wet and sputtering survivors were robbed. A few were murdered for their gold before a unit of the California Guard arrived on the scene to keep order.

In all, some 415 lives and an unknown quantity of gold and other precious metals were lost in the *Yankee Blade* calamity. To this day pieces of the old ship occasionally wash up at Point Honda or nearby Point Arguello, but little gold has been found.

Navy Fleet Goes Down at Honda

Coincidentally, Point Honda was also the site of the worst peacetime naval disaster in U.S. history. It occurred in early September 1923, when a highly experienced U.S. Navy captain made a mistake not unlike the one the master of the *Yankee Blade* had made. Seven recently launched destroyers and twenty-three young seamen would pay the ultimate price for their commander's fatal error.

In all his years as an officer in the United States Navy, Capt. Edward Watson had never seen a fog as thick as the one that shrouded the California coast on the evening of September 8, 1923. Captain Watson was in overall command of a sizable flotilla of fourteen destroyers steaming southward from San Francisco en route to the large naval base at San Diego. The fighting ships had completed about half their journey and soon would be making a wide eastward turn around Points Arguello and Conception—or so Captain Watson believed. In vain, he peered into the dense fog, hoping to catch a glimpse of lighthouse beacons calling to him from these strategic points of land. Once he had them in view, he knew his ships could safely turn to port and enter the protected waters of the Santa Barbara Channel. But on this night, he would never see the lights.

Maintaining a precise military formation, the destroyers ran one behind the other about two minutes apart. Their nervous skippers waited for Captain Watson to give the order to change course. A Navy veteran with many years of service, Watson was a decisive commander, but that night, in that fog, he was hesitant. His radioman had received a confusing electronic signal from Point Arguello. The radio beacon indicated that Captain Watson's lead ship, the *Delphy*, was still north of the point. If this were true, then what lay to the east

Behind the USS Chauncey *(DD-296), the USS* Young *(DD-312) is shown rolled over. The wreck occurred on September 8, 1923, in heavy fog.* Naval Historical Center, courtesy of the Collection of Edward C. Knapp, Sr., loaned by John E. Knapp

was not the safe water of the Santa Barbara Channel but rather a solid wall of ship-killing rocks.

There had been a second, conflicting radio signal received that night—one indicating that the flotilla was, indeed, about to enter the channel. Captain Watson weighed the information he had received and made a fateful decision. He would ignore both radio signals and rely on an old sailor's gut instincts. Navigating by dead reckoning, he plotted the flotilla's position and course. Then he gave his ships their orders and, one by one, they turned to port.

As it turned out, Captain Watson's instincts had failed him, and his flotilla was still far from the channel. The screams of metal—and men—could be heard as the *Delphy* struck the coast at a place called Honda, about a mile north of Point Arguello. Then, one after another, six more destroyers—the *Lee,* the *Young,* the *Woodbury,* the *Chauncey,* the *Nicholas,* and the *Fuller*—followed the *Delphy* to their doom. The other ships in the flotilla managed to bear off in time to avert disaster, but the seven at the head of the column were lost. Grinding to a halt on the rocks, they were torn apart by the pounding surf. In all, twenty-three sailors were lost in the mishap. The toll might have been much higher if not for the rescue efforts organized by keepers from the Point Arguello Lighthouse.

Located on a barren cliff almost 100 feet above the Pacific waves, the Point Arguello Station had been established in 1901. Its beacon helped mark the strategic rocky elbow where California's generally north-south trending coastline angles sharply back toward the east. Exposed and isolated, the lighthouse was never a popular duty station for keepers. It remained in operation only until 1934, when it was replaced by an automated light on an iron skeleton tower. Shortly after it was decommissioned, the old tower and residence was razed. Like Captain Watson's ill-fated flotilla, the lighthouse is now only a ghostly memory.

Coincidentally, one of Captain Watson's destroyers sank atop the wreck of the *Yankee Blade*. Salvagers taking brass and iron from the later wreck also pulled up parts of the *Blade,* including the ship's bell.

CHAPTER 3

The Colorado Changes Course
MAKING OF THE SALTON SEA
- 1905 -

"The main affair of life is to get the dollar, and if there is any money in cutting the throat of Beauty, why, by all means, cut her throat."

—John C. Van Dyke
The Desert

THE MIGHTY COLORADO RIVER TRAVELS A FAR distance to bring its water to the ocean. Starting out in Wyoming, it meanders through Colorado, Utah, and Arizona, until it passes

Flooded railroad in Coachella County in 1905. Coachella Valley Historical Society

through the Southern California desert named after it and on through Mexico to the Gulf of California. In its waters can be found the natural and unnatural substances of the lands it passes through, bringing both the goodness of the soils it traverses and runoff from farms and ranches that abut the river's banks. And as the water flows into the desert, those particles, both good and bad, come to rest.

The river has a natural flow, a movement east and west within its channel. The water carves its way more and more to the east until it cannot carve in that direction anymore. Then, on its own volition, the water begins to move west, always staying in its riverbed. When it cannot move in that direction anymore, it repeats the cycle.

In 1905 the Colorado had reached its farthest limits to the east and was preparing to move to the west again. But two factors would change the river forever: Heavy rains came to the west during the winters of 1905 and 1906, and, at the same time, a human endeavor to green the Colorado Desert (now the Imperial Valley) by using the river's waters to reclaim the arid lands for farming made an awful mistake.

The Colorado River's changing course through Southern California and Mexico to the Gulf of California, which could deviate by miles within its natural channel, fooled explorers and settlers for centuries. Maps dating back to the 1500s, when Spain first conquered the area, were found to be significantly off in the seventeenth century; those maps, in turn, were found to be wrong in the Mexican period in the 1800s, as they were in the American occupation that followed. By the turn of the twentieth century, the Colorado's quirky behavior had been documented enough to know not to trust what was plainly before one's eyes.

The Colorado Desert occasionally saw floods and collections of water for brief periods. The Cahuilla, Native Americans living in the area, would move away when they spotted unexpected pools of water collecting in the desert, a sure sign of imminent flooding. When the floods came to an end and the water disappeared, the Cahuilla would return to the area to eke out what they could from this otherwise barren land.

These floods were caused primarily by the overflow of water from the Colorado into smaller dry riverbeds such as the New and the Alamo Rivers, which traversed the valley floor. Such floods left pools of water for a while, which nourished travelers, such as the forty-niners, who passed through this desert on their way to California to prospect for gold in the mid-nineteenth century. But when whites came to live in the area, they were neither as observant as the long-suffering locals nor interested in knowing what the locals knew. They built where they wanted to live, expecting to settle in for a long time. Unexpected water collections were dismissed as unimportant until the floods of 1891 came through and washed away their assets.

During the 1870s the Southern Pacific Rail Road had built a rail line through the valley that gave rise to small towns along its route through the Salton Sink, the lowest point of land in the United States. A salt "farm" was doing great production there, and there were some hardy souls attempting to make something out of the heat and sun. But for the most part, the area was seen as something to pass through from Yuma, Arizona, and the mines along the Colorado to the temperate California coast.

So there was a real paradox here: a barren desert in which few people could live, bounded on its eastern end by a mighty and dangerous river whose waters could, if properly diverted, make the land an agricultural paradise. To some, such as the adventurers that the untamed West had lured from the staid eastern states, redirecting and redesigning nature offered the possibility of power and wealth that was just too tempting to ignore.

The floods of 1891 should have been a sign that the problems of diverting and controlling the Colorado were more complex than they seemed. The heavy rains that winter had caused both the Colorado and Gila Rivers to overflow their banks and destroy the Walnut

Grove Dam, swamping the town of Yuma, Arizona, and creating a temporary lake in the deepest part of the valley to the west, inside the Salton Sink. The owners of the salt beds were alarmed by the sudden departure of workers (mostly Cahuilla Indians) to higher elevations when the lake first formed. Since it was believed that white men could not endure the desert heat—only Native American, Mexican, and Japanese men worked in suffocating temperatures that rose as high as 140 degrees—salt production came to a halt. And the floods alarmed the townspeople of Yuma, because their lifeline was endangered should the lake become too large and swallow the tracks of the railroad.

Yet by the end of the decade, the floods were merely a bad memory, and newer arrivals with visions of great wealth from these lands neither knew nor cared about barriers to their success. One of those men was Charles Rockwood, a former University of Michigan engineering student who had quit school to seek his fortune in the rugged and wild West. His aborted training made him valuable to many, including the railroads and the government, and in 1892 he was hired by private investors to survey the land east of the Colorado River in the state of Sonora, Mexico. While he found these lands to be valueless, he realized that the lands to the west on both sides of the international border held great potential. He went back to his investors and asked for funding to do a survey of these lands. Granted in 1893, Rockwood's survey went into limbo when the Panic of 1893 wiped out his investors. Rockwood began complex and complicated dealings with the owner of the company, and in 1896 he took control of the Colorado River Irrigation Company and changed its name to the California Development Company (CDC). He was now in a position to pursue his dream of wealth and fortune in the deserts of the Imperial Valley.

Because of the difficulties of moving water past the Algodones Dunes, which stood between the river and the desert, Rockwood's plan was to divert the water at a point 12 miles north of Yuma called

Potholes, send it south by canal into Mexico, and then head it north and east into the United States. To do so he had to get the rights of way or acquire ownership of land in both countries, a gargantuan effort that caused him to use money he did not have and to beg for support from every possible investor in the United States, Mexico, and Europe that he could reach. Finally, Rockwood and his partner in this endeavor, Anthony Heber, secured the promise of funds from Hamilton Trust Company on February 14, 1898, only to find the next morning that the USS *Maine* had been blown up in Havana Harbor, ushering in the Spanish-American War. The planned support never arrived.

In 1899 Rockwood met with George Chaffey, world renowned for his irrigation projects in California and Canada. He, too, had believed that white men could not live in such hot climates until the Australian government hired him to build irrigation in Mildura and Adelaide, areas of great heat. There he saw whites working in the over-one-hundred-degree heat. But the projects failed, and he returned hungry for redemption. He believed he had found it in the CDC's plan to irrigate the Colorado Desert.

Chaffey made a deal with Rockwood, effectively taking control of the CDC, only to find that Rockwood's representation of the assets of the company was sheer fabrication. He had been led to believe that the company held rights to land and rights of way in two countries when it owned nothing; in fact it owed thousands of dollars to both private and governmental agencies. But Chaffey was driven by his own desire for redemption and the rewards thereof, and, instead of withdrawing from the plan, he took the bull by the horns. He made several changes, protected what assets there were, demoted Rockwood to assistant engineer of one of the proposed projects, and started moving toward his goal of conquering the desert.

Certainly, Chaffey and Rockwood were not the only people trying to control nature in this part of the West. Throughout all of these years, others had tried to invest in the land and its development, forming uneasy and constantly shifting alliances that would control planned towns and properties. But Chaffey was a doer, and he went into action as quickly as he could.

Chaffey built a temporary cut, or headgate, into the Colorado River on the American side of the border near the southern tip of the Algodones Dunes, known as Hanson's Gate, that allowed the water to be diverted into a canal that paralleled the river as it traveled in Mexico. When it reached the Alamo River, it was diverted west to a canal 40 miles away that would head it north back into the United States at what is now Calexico, a town named by Chaffey to symbolize the international nature of the project. In May 1901 the first water was diverted successfully, ushering in the beginning of what would become an agricultural bonanza and an ecological disaster.

So, by violating private property rights, by privatizing water that was freely flowing in a publicly owned river, by undermining the laws of two countries, Chaffey, Rockwood, and others started their sales of water rights to the new, unsuspecting settlers of what Chaffey named the Imperial Valley. It wasn't that all of this hadn't been done before in other parts of the country or to the laws of either country, but it had never been done on this scale or with such audacity as these men showed.

So the CDC provided a service: They brought the water to the land. Buying water made the useless land valuable. Water was made available to the local water distributors (which the CDC owned and operated) at a high price; the distributors then sold the water and delivered it to the farms for a higher price. But to be able to purchase the water, the settler needed to own the land. That was done through the Desert Land Act or the Homestead Act, which permitted a claim of 160 acres or 320 acres, depending on the law under which the settler filed. To meet the legal requirement of improving the land, a part of the process by which an individual would obtain ownership, the settler bought shares in the CDC-owned local water company so they could receive water. But the CDC had sold the shares to investors at a discount to stay afloat in earlier years; now these investors were selling shares through auctions at fluctuating prices. And still the settlers, after having paid enormous amounts for the shares, had to buy the water at a high price! (And we thought Enron was the originator of such schemes.)

Chaffey eventually was forced out of the company through the stock manipulations of Rockwood and Heber, who had again joined forces. He took a third of the value of his $300,000 in assets and said good-bye to the desert forever after building 400 miles of canals and a water empire in less than two years. And while the federal government worried about the size of the abuse of the laws of the land, the CDC continued to exploit the settlers of the valley and plan new ways to deliver water to an ever-growing population.

The Imperial Valley was becoming an important agricultural area of California, spawning the development of many crops, including sugar beet, sorghum, and other heat-resistant vegetables and plants. But if the water system failed, the valley would turn back to alkaline dust.

While the CDC had successfully built canals and delivered water to thousands of acres of land, the company began to experience setbacks. In 1902 the Department of Agriculture claimed that the land being irrigated was too alkaline to continue to produce crops, which scared farmers and investors alike. While the department pulled back significantly from this position later (a view that has been proven over the years to be incorrect), the CDC suffered a bad blow to its reputation. At the same time the Justice Department started to look into the legality of the CDC setup.

But Chaffey's and, later, Rockwood's cost-cutting measures were the real problem. When building the original headgate, Chaffey had created a temporary structure at the wrong depth, and he warned

Rockwood to replace it. Rockwood, watching investors depart in the face of the damaging Agriculture Department report, let it go. The silt built up in the canal and eventually cut off the water supply. Rockwood tried many methods to get the water to run again, but he failed. Finally, at a point of desperation, farmers started to sue the CDC when water failed to arrive in a timely fashion. Rockwood decided to start over by building another headgate and canal.

Right about this time, the U.S. government established a program of "reclaiming" or finding uses for land that had been deemed to be unsuitable for agriculture. The Reclamation Service, a division of the U.S. Geological Survey, had been given the task of determining which arid lands were eligible and designing a workable plan of action to use the existing natural resources in a way that would be beneficial to the country. Land could be worked for its mineral rights, for instance, or it could be eligible for irrigation for agriculture. The designation of irrigable land is based on a survey, which quantifies the acreage and its natural elements—minerals, quality of soil, access to water, rainfall amounts, and other qualities—that will then be used to plan an irrigation system and create a new physical map of the old natural landscape. Dams and irrigation systems that will bring water into the area are built, usually by industry but at times by the government, to meet the specifications of the plan.

The Reclamation Service released a plan to irrigate the Colorado Desert, including the Imperial Valley, at no cost to the farmers, with an integrated system of irrigation canals, reservoirs, and dams. Now the farmers, who had paid a high price to get water from the CDC, although wary of government interference, asked themselves the obvious question, "Why pay for water that is not being delivered when we can get it delivered for free?"

Rockwood and Heber, realizing that they had lost the battle with the U.S. government, turned to Mexico for help. Rockwood opened a hole in the banks of the Colorado River 4 miles south of the border and sent water into a 7-foot-deep path to the Imperial Canal at a point south of the silted up area, and once again water flowed freely to the valley. But Rockwood did nothing to protect his new canal, waiting, he claimed, for the Mexican government to approve his construction plans. Meanwhile the Colorado River and runoff from a couple of El Niño winters prepared to take their tolls.

Fortunes are made and lost through a mixture of skill and luck. Rockwood, it could be concluded, had neither. The years of 1905 and 1906 turned out to be the rainiest in the Rocky Mountains, from which the Colorado collects runoff as it meanders to the Gulf of California, and the wettest in centuries in this area of Southern California. The flood of February 1905 caused the Colorado to swell as never before seen by whites.

With no gate to protect Rockwood's cut in the Colorado wall, the onrushing water not only flowed out through the hole in its wall but increased the size of the hole dramatically. The little ditch that Rockwood had built to carry water to the Imperial Canal was unable to handle the excess water, which quickly overflowed its banks and headed north and west toward the international border back into the United States.

But with an ever-shifting river channel, the Colorado, which had been on the eastern side of its own migration cycle, quickly took advantage of the opening. It headed west, making the new cut, now dangerously enlarged, into its main channel, abandoning its centuries-old southward path to the Gulf for the ease of this new western flow. A once-thriving ecology, based on the permanence of the river's presence, was suddenly shocked to death by its sudden departure.

The February flood, although unexpected (since floods usually occurred in the summer along the Colorado), may have been a cleansing action for the farmers upstream, but when the waters receded, Rockwood found that his channel had a new deposit of silt, which he attempted to excavate. But a second flood followed soon thereafter, and again Rockwood attempted to dredge his canal in anticipation of the summer floods.

It was only after the third flood in less than a month, on March 3, 1905, that Rockwood realized the possibilities of an extremely wet season. Figuring the CDC gates up north of the border would be usable in that kind of a situation, he ordered the Mexican cut to be closed. But his attempts to close the hole were futile, as a fourth flood and then a fifth slammed into his breach.

And with this series of floods, the river redirected itself into a tiny channel and headed west and north back into the United States. Water, when left to its own devices, will always seek the lowest point it can find. Given that there was nothing to stop it until it found its lowest point, the water kept going, until it reached the lowest point in the valley, and the United States, the Salton Sink. But the water, which had first flooded and receded, no longer ebbed and flowed; it only flowed, at levels as fast as 120,000 cubic feet per second, into the valley, wiping out towns, businesses and farms, rail lines, and anything else in its path to the Sink.

For the next two years, this low basin would continue to gather up the Colorado into its fold, giving the water a place to settle on the alkaline desert, a new home all its own. And it took the mightiest of the masters of industry and much of the resources he had at his disposal to end this environmental disaster.

Edward Harriman controlled many of the railroads in the United States. He ran the Southern Pacific and the Union Pacific, as well as other smaller lines and related industries. When the CDC, which had turned everywhere for help and had been rebuffed, first asked Harriman for help, he too turned them down. But Rockwood and his associates persisted, and, for reasons known only to him, Harriman had a change of heart. That is, if he had a heart at all. Calculated risk was his game, and he was very good at it. And the CDC was desperate, willing to do just about anything to hold on.

Harriman seized the situation, believing that the wealth of land the CDC controlled, especially the land held in Mexico, would be worth risking a couple of hundred thousand dollars for. He proposed to loan the money in exchange for control of the board of directors of the CDC and a Harriman choice for president of the company. By placing the company's stock in trust, the loan would be collateralized, meaning that if the company made a profit, so would Harriman, and if the company failed, he would get the company's stock and own it. At a planned stockholders meeting, Rockwood and his associates ousted Heber from the board, agreed to Harriman's conditions, and received $200,000 to fix a hole in the Colorado's wall.

By that time, early summer, the Colorado was again flooding, but now the spring runoff from the mountains had come to the southern portion of the river. The force of the water had widened the Mexican cut to about 160 feet, dashing early hopes of relatively easy ways to close the gap. The new CDC president, Epes Randolph, an engineer himself, believed that closing the opening would be extremely difficult without more resources. Harriman agreed—and all of the power and strength of the Southern Pacific would be needed to end this nightmare.

Randolph allowed Rockwood to continue to lead the operation to redivert the river into its original pathways. Rockwood first attempted to build a levee off a sandbar island, hoping to redirect the course of the river toward the east, but the pilings, made of brush and barbed wire, became increasingly difficult to drive into the riverbed, because the river's current increased as the space in which it could flow was decreased. Finally, Rockwood abandoned this plan and turned to the idea of another bypass with a properly constructed floodgate. In coordination with the opening of a permanent replacement for the original silt-filled canal gate north of Yuma, this new gate would control the river and would eventually allow for the damming of the open gap in Mexico.

Meanwhile, the water continued to gather in the Sink, flooding first the New Liverpool Salt Company's farms, then threatening the Southern Pacific rail line. While Rockwood was away in Los Angeles on company business, the plans to build a new gate were abandoned by Randolph and his superintendent of bridges, E. S. Edinger. Instead, the materials were used to construct a jetty nearby in the hopes that it could stop the river before it overtook the railroad tracks. But little could have withstood the force of the water that came down the Colorado and the Gila on November 29 and 30, 1905, which tore away the jetty and just about anything else in its way. When that event ended, the gap had grown to 600 feet!

The Sink was filling fast with the river's water. What was worse, the slope of the new path of the river was greater than the slope of its path to the sea, making it even more difficult to convince the river to return to its original course. Fear spread throughout the valley that this disaster might never end. After swallowing the salt farm, the water came up to the tracks, which at that point were moved to higher elevations and later again to an even higher point. And with the river came all of the detritus that it had swept up on the way to its new home.

Rockwood then attempted a new and bigger gate farther west of the river's edge, and during the low-flow winter months, work proceeded. At the same time, another gate was being constructed north of Yuma. But Randolph had finally come to the end of his rope with the man in charge of the project, and by late April, Rockwood was gone. Still, time caught up with the operations, and the summer floods came before the work was finished.

Even in the face of this expensive failure, even as San Francisco—a major Southern Pacific and Union Pacific rail hub—rocked and burned in its great earthquake and fire, Harriman decided not to give up. He authorized another $250,000, and Randolph placed Henry Thomas Cory—a former engineering professor working for Southern Pacific—in charge of the operation.

The 1906 summer floods took the Imperial Valley to a new level of destruction. The river's flow went from fast water over rapids to drops of as much as 80 feet on its way to the Salton basin. The original riverbed to the Gulf was starting to sprout desert flora as the gap that was stealing its water grew larger, to almost 3,000 feet. The new flow itself was a mile wide, its overflow ran into formerly dry creeks and riverbeds, destroying the very canals that the CDC itself had built for irrigation. That destruction meant that the land once irrigated was now returning to its desert form. And still the water came, and still the Sink filled.

A controlled hysteria came to the valley and other desert communities like Yuma. The great fear was that the river could never be diverted, that the opening would grow even wider, and the Colorado Desert would disappear into a vast sea, taking with it the hopes, dreams, and investments of the now-thousands of settlers.

The floods threatened and then consumed town after town, taking the dirt and debris with it to the basin. The fight to save Calexico, the town Chaffey had built along the northern side of the border that was the home of the offices of the CDC, was a particularly poignant and ironic event. While the townspeople mustered all they had, to the point even of moving the Southern Pacific rail depot to higher ground and diverting the waters through dynamiting, the losses not only included the assets of the locals but also the destruction of most of Mexicali, its Mexican twin city not a mile away.

Cory brought in dozens of engineers to survey and propose ways to stop the disaster. When none could agree, Cory came up with his own plan. Up until then, Harriman and his associates had taken half measures in the fight. Cory's answer was so great a vision that it would require a tremendous investment and the focused energy of the mighty railroad parent to pull it off. Even then, there was only a slim chance to beat the river back to its original route to the sea.

The first thing was to build a rail spur from the mainline that followed the river's bank down to the opening of the Mexican gap or crevasse. Placed at Cory's disposal was the equivalent of a small railroad company, everything from locomotives to freight cars that could move fifty tons at a time. The CDC itself had a few boats and several barges, and the coal needed to run all these engines.

Rock fill was brought in from quarries within a 400-mile radius of the valley, thousands of linear feet of timber from northern California, clay from nearby parts of Mexico, gravel from north of the border, steel wire measured by the dozens of miles—and all the equipment necessary to work the rock fill into the needed shapes and sizes and to pile and drive the fill into the broken bank of the errant river.

Cory used the name and status of the Southern Pacific to bring hundreds of skilled workmen, from engineers to equipment operators, and built a small city as headquarters. He brought in a workforce of more than a thousand Native Americans from throughout the Southwest and Mexicans from the local area, and an army of others to provide necessary services. Food, housing, tools, clothing, medicine, and medical facilities were all brought together for this massive undertaking. The Mexican government was asked to declare martial law and police the area, to keep differences among the various tribes and between white and Mexican workers from turning into violence.

Steel-wire cable was used to bind the brush that would be placed down first as a foundation for the quarry rock. Without that foundation the fear was that the rocks would just sink into the sandy bottom under the river. The crews assembled the bundles in about three weeks. Using boats and barges to drag out this half-mile long "mattress," it was sunk to the bottom of the gap in the embankment at the end of August 1906.

Then a bridge was built out above the end of the embankment so that the freight trains could bring the rock, gravel, and clay into the channel. But the whole operation was predicated on the belief that the Rockwood gate would hold. On October 11, however, the gate collapsed, creating a new main channel for the river to follow. With the Hanson gate north of Yuma finished and opened, boxcars of rock began to be piled up along the embankment. The gap was closed on November 4.

Everything went along fine for about a month, when on December 7, a surge in the river's flow dissolved the CDC-built banks that masqueraded as levees nearby. The river was once again on the loose. Out of control, the Colorado moved as it saw fit, much to the dismay of Southern Pacific engineers and to the terror of valley residents.

There was little time to lose. This surge had not been predicted, which meant that another could happen at any time, regardless of the history of dry winters and wet summers. And even if they fixed the present hole, any part of the levee that had been built by the CDC was suspect to future breaches. All of it would have to be replaced.

Harriman's attempts to get money from the federal government to do this work were rebuffed, first by Theodore Roosevelt and then by Congress. He turned back to Cory the responsibility of ending this water and cash flood. And Cory took Southern Pacific to new heights in this fight to convince the river that it wanted to return to its original path.

Cory, after three unsuccessful attempts, finally built a trestle bridge across the open embankment that would allow trains to dump their rock, gravel, and clay loads (and anything else that could help sustain the wall). Starting on January 27, 1907, trainload after trainload arrived, dumped its load, and departed to get more. All train service was temporarily halted out of Los Angeles as every available engine and useful car was put into service. The idea was to build up the riverbank along its west side high enough (a minimum of 11 feet) that would make the path of least resistance the original channel, abandoned once again in the latest levee failure. Slowly—excruciatingly slowly to the settlers as well as the Southern Pacific hierarchy—the river was forced to change its course. On February 10, nearly two years and almost $3 million later, the river returned to its normal channel and flowed on to the Gulf of California.

But what of the water that had flooded the valley? What would become of this new sea, the Salton Sea, which stretched for 38 miles over a swath 15 miles wide?

At first many believed that the water would evaporate in the heat of the desert, that the sea would be gone in fourteen years, if that long. The errant river had carved a new face on old riverbeds, making them natural channels for irrigation and its wastewater to flow down. And while the Salton Sea had lost its major source of intake, what intake it got would be the unused water and the runoff sewage of the agricultural fields and towns that grew up around it. While the sea at first shrank, it eventually evened out with the natural ebb and flow of its own stability. Having no outflow of its own except evaporation, new water maintained its relative size, a growth-and-shrinkage limit of 15 feet of depth.

In less than ten years, the valley had turned a definite shade of green and transformed into a major agricultural center. And the Salton Sea, the orphaned child of the Colorado River's wild ride through the Imperial Valley, was now reminiscent of a gigantic septic tank, unable to sustain life from its naturally alkaline mixture.

When the river first left its banks and dried up its old channel, those animals capable of following, namely waterfowl, did so. While game birds left due to a lack of food soon after the water migration ended, others stayed, as varied as cormorants and puffins and phalaropes and sandpipers, along with great blue herons, gulls, and pelicans. At present close to four hundred species of birds habituate the area—some far from their usual haunts, but many others were those who had regularly come to the local lakes and occasionally appearing puddles that arose from time to time before the disaster. The Salton Sea has become a vital part of the western flyway, and the government has christened it a national wildlife refuge in recognition of this fact.

But the Salton Sea is a refuge for disease as well. Tens of thousands of birds—sometimes in epidemic proportions—die each year along the banks of this polluted alkaline lake. And the pollution into the Salton Sea continues to this day, multiplying the problems of high salt and organic matter with measurable levels of toxic chemicals and minerals. Few fish survive the Salton toxicity, although recently four species, including tilapia that had been introduced into the canals to eat weeds, have flourished.

Two sidelights of note to the story of the Salton Sea:

First is the damage to the ecosystem of the Colorado River Delta, the area that lost its water for over two years. While the river returned to its proper channel, some of the wetlands it supported could not be revived. Bird populations as well as fish species, and farther down into the Gulf of California, shrimp and other seafood catches, have all declined dramatically.

The second is what happened to the local Native American populations. Granted land in the Salton Sink in the 1890s and then again after the sea developed, the irony of the government's grant of land to a band of the Cahuilla Nation has placed this group on the edge of great wealth. The Imperial Irrigation District (IID), formed in 1911 to represent the water interests of the now-Imperial County landowners, began to buy up as much of the land as possible around and under the malformed sea from former deed holders, including the Southern Pacific Railroad rights-of-way. The district then used the Salton Sea as the sump of the county, pouring its effluvia into the lake indiscriminately. But the government sued the IID for damages for misuse of the Indian lands. In a settlement that's still pending, the Indians chose to receive equivalent land (drier for sure) near Palm Springs in the hopes of opening a casino. Other casino operators, including other Native Americans, have tried to halt this arrangement, for fear of losing income at their own gaming houses.

In the end the sea of human error has gained permanence in the

Imperial Valley. But just as a more systematic plunder of the Colorado River has transformed the desert, so the existence of that inland empire is dependent on exacting controls of its environment. The Salton Sea now plays a vital role in this new Imperial Valley, as it gives harbor to animals that should not be there and refuge to the waste of the farms and towns that should not be there. Rockwood's legacy, if we can call it that, is established for all times. The Salton Sea lives on in his memory, a monument to greed and incompetence and a shrine to how the West was won.

CHAPTER 4
Terror in San Francisco
EARTHQUAKE AND FIRE
- 1906 -

THE YEAR 1906 WAS NOT A GOOD ONE FOR CALIFORNIA. Already into the second year of the floods caused by the Colorado River in the south, the northern part of the state was shocked into terror at 5:13 A.M. on Wednesday, April 18. At that moment one tectonic plate deep below the surface of the earth moved north-northwest against another tectonic plate moving southward. The force of this movement heaved the earth's crust above along a 10-mile-wide strip

The San Francisco earthquake was estimated as 7.9 on the Richter scale — estimated because the seismometers broke with the force of the temblor.
California Office of Emergency Services

of the Pacific coast, creating a rift that ranged from 9 feet to 30 feet. The rupture itself ran from San Juan Battista to Cape Mendocino, a distance of 270 miles.

The shockwaves were felt as far away as Los Angeles, Oregon, and Nevada and by ships 150 miles out in the Pacific Ocean. On farms, buildings were moved several feet, generating stories of the earth swallowing up a barn as it opened and then reclosed. Great redwoods were heaved as their roots were torn from the ground. Ironically, the greatest destruction of trees took place at Loma Prieta in the Santa Cruz Mountains, which would become the epicenter of the 1989 temblor.

The most severe damage was done to San Francisco, a city of some 450,000 people. San Francisco had become a cultural, industrial, financial, and political center for the western United States, and it had grown from a few dozen people to a thriving metropolis. San Francisco's leaders saw it as the future center for the Pacific Rim, and had begun to build structures reminiscent of French Beaux-Arts and Roman architecture as would befit a capital. At its opera house on the night before the devastation, Enrico Caruso and the Metropolitan Opera Company from New York had stunned the audience with a magnificent performance of *Carmen*, and John Barrymore's touring company had just presented *The Dictator*, in which he starred.

And while the area had experienced earthquakes before—an even greater one had occurred in 1838, eight years before the United States took possession of Yerba Buena, the Mexican village later renamed for St. Francis of Assisi—few had been there to have been bothered. More than 200 earthquakes had been felt during the city's fifty-year American period, but no one was prepared for one of this magnitude.

Not that worries about safety did not exist in the city. San Francisco had burned to the ground a few times in its early years, and over the decades the residents developed volunteer fire companies to keep the city from burning again. Finally, the city had created a professional

Caruso's Curse

The great tenor Enrico Caruso had chosen to perform in San Francisco after canceling scheduled performances in his native Italy. His decision was based on reports that Mt. Vesuvius, the volcano in whose shadow Naples rested, was about to blow. And it did. Caruso congratulated himself on his decision, and he performed on the eve of the earthquake in what is considered one of his greatest performances.

Caruso said later that when the earthquake hit he felt that the demons of Naples had pursued him across the ocean and continent. Confused and frightened, his conductor rushed into his room and, at the window looking out at the great destruction, hearing the cries of people for help, urged Caruso to sing, to show that he was not afraid and that his voice was undamaged. And Caruso did, as San Francisco shook and burned, as people around him jumped from windows and ran from falling debris. Reminiscent of Nero, who fiddled while Rome burned, Caruso sang.

---

firefighting agency, and, ironically, on the very day of the earthquake, the proposal to protect San Francisco from the loss of its water supply for firefighting was going to be heard by the city's leadership.

Downtown San Francisco is laid out on a grid. Between the Ferry Building and Twin Peaks, with Market Street as its diagonal dividing line, the area to the north was a generally neat block pattern contoured to the steep hills the city is known for, with occasional squares for people to gather; the area to the south of Market was a distinctly different pattern on a flat expanse of land, a place where many industries and workers resided.

The earthquake, generally considered to have had a force equivalent to a magnitude 7.9 on the Richter scale (although it is just an estimate, because the seismometers broke with the force of the temblor) lasted fifty seconds, according to most accounts. The shaking knocked down many buildings, especially in the heavily populated South of Market area, killing and maiming many residents.

But that was not the worst of it. The real damage was underground, where the heaving earth ruptured gas lines and water pipes. The gas ignited almost immediately, and flames started to rush through the tinderbox tenement houses south of Market. In other parts of the city, other fires started. And while there was plenty of water stored for firefighting purposes, without the pipes to move the water from their reservoirs, and without pumps to move the water through the pipes, there might be no stopping the fires as they grew and moved, consuming everything they could as they crawled toward downtown.

If that were not enough, a severe aftershock hit at 8:14 A.M., and the level of panic grew even greater. Those who had survived the first shake looked for ways to leave. But the quake had also destroyed cable car lines, twisting the steel rails as if they were rubber. Streets themselves had been heaved so badly that many were impassable. The telephone system had collapsed, as had the telegraph. "Not in history has a modern imperial city been so completely destroyed," wrote Jack London, who came from his home in Oakland across San Francisco Bay to witness the disaster.

The flames drew the winds, which came from all directions to feed and move the fire from one source of fuel to another, from building to building, from house to house. Buildings that had survived the quake were dynamited in the hopes that their destruction would minimize the amount of fuel available. Yet, another block, and then another block, and still another block were consumed.

At first most of the quake damage was south of Market, which housed the workers of the city, and in the financial and business district, which had been built on landfill (on the site of hundreds of scuttled boats that had brought the forty-niners during the Gold Rush). On Nob Hill the wealthy looked out over the city, gathering to watch the black smoke rising from the tenements. To them the fire was a spectacle that would eventually burn itself out; it would never reach the high and mighty perched upon the hill.

But other fires around the city were also out of control, and the fire department, whose chief died in the quake itself, was disorganized, as each unit tried to stop local fires without water and without a centralized plan. Ironically, there were reports of some buildings being set on fire purposely, because the owners' insurance policies did not cover earthquake damage but did pay on fire.

Hundreds were caught up in the South of Market fire, burned to death—to char—in a matter of moments. Most were never found or identified. As the flames progressed through the district, survivors packed what belongings they could drag or carry and fled. Tens of thousands moved themselves toward the north, then west, to get out of the way of the oncoming flames.

Gen. Frederick Funston, temporarily in command of the armed forces stationed in San Francisco's Fort Mason and at the Presidio, sent his soldiers to report to Mayor Eugene E. Schmitz—a controversial decision because it was a clear violation of the U.S. Constitution. The mayor sent the troops to patrol the fire line and to keep people moving away, even if it meant leaving their possessions behind, to escape the flames. The line retreated block by block as the flames took more and more of the flatlands and started to creep toward the hills housing the well-to-do.

The strength of the strongest worker flagged on San Francisco's steep hills, and many belongings were left behind as the flames caught up with these sudden refugees. According to Jack London, some dug holes and buried their possessions, hoping to return to them after the fire had abated.

On Wednesday evening the fire had yet to reach the business and

This panoramic view from the Stanford Mansion site looking toward Grace Church shows the extent of the city's destruction caused by both earthquake and fire.

financial districts north of Market Street. But it would be only a matter of hours before the converging paths of smaller fires jumped Market Street and devoured those buildings as well. With only dynamite, brooms, and blankets to stifle the flames, the area was abandoned. San Francisco's residents, the refugees, the soldiers, and the city's fathers waited for the inevitable to happen.

There were those who panicked and wandered without purpose and those who took advantage of a chaotic situation. The dazed and confused were found and looked after by relief agencies. But looting began, and almost immediately Mayor Schmitz declared that looters were to be shot on sight. The order was taken seriously. Later investigations showed that more than 500 civilians were shot for the slightest infraction, often left on the streets with signs on them stating their misdemeanor, offered to the fire or left as food for rats. And while looters were shot, many later testified that soldiers and militia themselves participated in the looting, without penalty, of course. Alcohol topped the list of what was being stolen, and out-of-control

Library of Congress

soldiers broke into saloons and stores to help themselves to whisky. Once drunk, these soldiers went on looting rampages, and many shot groups of homeless for sport.

The use of indoor stoves was banned, because, with so many chimneys fallen in the quake, closed or blocked flues would ignite new fires. The consequences of chimney fires became a reality for those in the area of City Hall. A woman decided to prepare a breakfast of ham and eggs for her family, not realizing that her chimney was blocked. Igniting the gas fire set the house on fire, which started one of the largest fires in the city. Known as the Ham and Eggs Fire, it eventually burned the already wrecked City Hall, St. Ignatius Church, the Hall of Justice, Mechanics Pavilion (which had been turned into an emergency hospital), and other important structures southwest of downtown. Residents in unburned areas moved their stoves out onto the street to cook.

The army and later the National Guard were assigned the task of patrolling the streets, while the city police moved people and bodies.

With City Hall nearly destroyed, the mayor moved city government to the Hall of Justice until it, too, was about to be overwhelmed by the oncoming flames. The mayoral offices moved to Fort Mason once the fires were put out.

The mayor, who before the quake had expected to be brought up on extortion charges as part of a sweep of the graft-ridden city government, decided that he could get some good public relations out of the disaster by creating an advisory group of prominent citizens to lead the recovery efforts. To this group he appointed those who were leading the reform movement. His hope was that by putting trustworthy people in charge, the case against him would be dropped. The Committee of Fifty was formed, and James Phelan, one of Schmitz's major opponents and a former reform mayor himself, was put in charge.

The panic-stricken homeless got a reprieve when Edward Harriman, head of the Southern Pacific Railroad, offered anyone who wanted to leave a free ride on his railroad. While its San Francisco hub had been destroyed, the Southern Pacific also owned the ferries that traveled from the Ferry Building to link to trains in the East Bay. Ferries continued to move people out of San Francisco and onto waiting trains. Over the next nine days, the Southern Pacific moved nearly 300,000 people out of the Bay Area, 225,000 of them in the first five days. It was the largest evacuation performed to that time, subsequently surpassed only by Dunkirk at the beginning of World War II and New Orleans in the wake of Hurricane Katrina.

The military, in coordination with relief groups, also set up tent camps, first in Union Square and later in the Presidio and Golden Gate Park. Supplies came in as ships started to arrive, but before that soldiers were sent into abandoned stores to gather food, and church groups and nongovernmental agencies such as the Red Cross stepped in to feed the refugees and tend to the wounded.

Individual fires were rampant through the city. A fire that had broken out in the north end started moving to meet the two larger

San Franciscans fled the ruined city on horseback, in wagons, or, if they were lucky enough to own one, in newfangled automobiles. California Office of Emergency Services

fires coming from the south. Within hours the thousands who, thinking that they were safe from the blaze, had encamped in Union Square, were forced to evacuate as all sides of the square were in flames. Gone were the great buildings, such as the St. Francis Hotel, that surrounded the square.

Next to go was Chinatown, just to the north of Union Square. The fire that took this ghetto was started when police used black powder to explode buildings along Kearny Street, its eastern border. Set poorly and too late to starve the existing fire, these explosions sent burning cinder onto other buildings, which went up in flames. Tens of thousands of people were living in the nine-square-block area of Chinatown, forced to live there by the laws of San Francisco and California. Some never left, especially those women who had been brought in from China for prostitution. It is estimated today that more Chinese died in the conflagration than members of any other ethnic group. No white person's home would afford them comfort; they were hounded out of the area, and then looters took what they had left behind before the flames came. Even after the fire had burned out, looters returned to steal more assets from Chinatown businesses.

By Thursday morning the flames had engulfed the eastern and southern slopes of Nob Hill, home to the men who had made their money from the Gold Rush, the Comstock Lode, and the railroads. Those who had watched smugly as the fires burned on the plains below went from riches to rags as, one by one, the hungry fire ate their gaudy palaces. By Friday, April 20, not one of these structures stood standing.

The sky, filled with black smoke, turned daylight into darkness. The sun, when it could be seen, was a red ball against the dark cloud, and where blue sky could be seen, the prism effect created magnificent patterns of color. And while the sky was blackened and the city burned, the ground continued to shake. In the first two days, 135 aftershocks were recorded.

Rats fled as well. Untold numbers left as buildings they had infested burned to the ground. Rats were a real menace, because they carried fleas that bore diseases such as the plague, threatening the lives of those who had survived the damage. Schmitz added the rats to his order to shoot on sight. It is estimated that 150,000 rodents were killed in San Francisco over the next ten days. In the end only 160 people were listed as having contracted the plague, of whom 77 died. However, only whites were included in that figure.

The refugees of the destruction kept moving westward as the fire lapped at their feet. By Thursday the fire had swept through the Barbary Coast and up Telegraph Hill on the northeast and up Nob Hill and Russian Hill to the northwest. The next line of defense to the west was Van Ness Avenue, a wide north-south thoroughfare beyond which few people lived. If the fire were to pass this point, there was no telling where it would stop; Fort Mason and the newly forested Presidio would be next, then Golden Gate Park, until finally the fire

Apparently parked outside a swank department store, this early steam-driven automobile was flattened by falling bricks and debris. California Office of Emergency Services

would reach the ocean's edge. Hundreds of thousands had moved to the safety of this area. Where would they go next?

The firefighters began by dynamiting the rest of the elegant mansions atop and along the western side of Nob Hill in an effort to destroy as many of them as possible before the fire consumed them as fuel, and to build a larger firebreak over which the flames would be unable to leap.

The fire had also moved south into the Mission District, threatening the quake-damaged Mission itself at Eighteenth Street and Dolores. But miraculously, one fire hydrant, at the corner of Twentieth and Mission Streets, still worked! Water was pumped and the firefighters were able to quash the flames, stopping the fire from consuming the rest of the Mission District and the Eureka Valley, today known as the Castro. The hydrant, which still works, receives a fresh coat of gold paint annually and remains a treasured monument to the rebirth of the city.

The attempt to set a backfire on the east side of Van Ness Avenue was a failure. Once again the stores of dynamite needed to start the backfire arrived too late. While some parts of the fire were halted at the avenue, at other spots the fire jumped over the street to start burning its way through the buildings of the Western Addition, a section of land holding thousands of refugees. Once again those homeless moved west to outrun the fire.

While the flames advanced in one small area six blocks past Van Ness, most of the fire was put out one block farther west at Franklin Street. Although the fire continued to burn, it had been contained. Or so they thought—until there was a huge explosion. The Viavi Building at the corner of Vallejo and Van Ness Avenue had been dynamited, though it didn't need to be. Its embers flew across Van Ness, sending the fire northward toward the North Beach docks.

Twenty thousand people had waited out the fire along these piers just east of Fort Mason. Panic set in as these refugees realized they were trapped. General Funston ordered in ships to evacuate them, and most were pulled out before the fire annihilated the northern docks.

This new fire then swept around the docks eastward and then southerly until it came back around to feed on already burned areas of the Barbary Coast and the financial district. The block now known as Jackson Square, left untouched by the original fire, was now in danger again. The firefighters and the local residents, standing on rooftops, fought off the fire. The navy stretched a mile-long hose to dowse the fire. Irony struck again, as the churches of San Francisco were laid to waste, but the warehouse of Hotaling Whisky was saved. (That area is the same as it was in 1906, and is thriving.)

However, now the fire was threatening the ferry docks and the warehouses along the eastern piers that had been untouched. The lifeline to the East Bay was in danger of being lost! Fireboats and naval vessels gathered around the Belvedere ferry dock for another

The city's debris was pushed into the bay at Golden Gate, near where the bridge with that name would be built thirty-one years later.

California Office of Emergency Services

stand against the flames. With the flames surrounded by water—including hoses from its land side manned by the firefighters in one last heroic effort—the fire was put out.

Meanwhile, fire was attempting to move west from Van Ness. Firefighters attacked using hoses that now stretched from the docking area near Fort Mason. And finally, the winds changed, moving the fire back upon itself until at 7:15 A.M. on Saturday, April 21, it was extinguished.

Although the official reports stated that there were only 498 deaths, investigation decades later estimated the toll at ten times that number. There are many stories from eyewitnesses of tenements filled with families and buildings filled with people hardly on the radar of the elite of the city collapsing in the earthquake and burning in the firestorm that followed. Indeed, there is testimony that mercy killings were performed. In one case, 350 of those with gravest injuries who were unable to be removed from the makeshift hospital in the Mechanics Pavilion to the outdoor triage in Golden Gate Park before the building burned, were said to have been sedated and then shot by soldiers. Police and soldiers killed others throughout the city who were trapped or pinned down by debris as the fires approached to keep them from further suffering. None of these accounts are part of the official record.

At the same time there are countless stories of heroism, of strangers going out of their way to help strangers as the earth opened up and burning cinders swirled around them. People ran into buildings to save lives, threatening their own. Soldiers gave up their own tents to the homeless.

The city was split in two as the fires started to burn out. The army was given the responsibility for the area west of Van Ness Avenue, which included the military bases and Golden Gate Park, the home to 200,000 homeless souls. The militia, police, and "irregulars," those civilians deputized by City Hall, were responsible for the burned-out eastern districts. An uneasy truce existed between these two groups, although at times both sides made forays into the other's area, ostensibly to bring order but more likely to establish their positions of authority.

But the earthquake and fire, now subdued, only led to the next disaster: relief woes. Aid poured in from throughout the country. Congress quickly appropriated a half-million dollars, and President Theodore Roosevelt, not trusting the army or the city's mayor, channeled it through the Red Cross. But that agency was ill equipped to handle this monumental task. The army was required to provide tents, food, medicine, and security to the homeless. Supplies disappeared

Neither rain, nor snow, nor earthquake? Despite the widespread destruction, temporary postal facilities like the tent at left ensured that San Francisco's mail continued to be delivered. California Office of Emergency Services

as the city grafters took their share; little actually got to those who needed it.

Eventually, those living in tents were able to rent, and later own, small houses built after the quake as permanent shelter. The city got rid of its corrupt mayor and began the downtown rebuilding process. Debris from the disaster was pushed into the bay to the east of the Golden Gate, where later a bridge would be built bearing that name. The area was—just as the area close to the Ferry Building near the foot of Market Street—filled until dirt hid the ruins of the nightmare. Houses and businesses soon were built above it. The Marina District's base would later play a part in another powerful earthquake, Loma Prieta, in 1989.

After the gaudy palaces, the rat-infested tenements, and the lascivious saloons of this once-wild city had been leveled, for a brief time all classes and races were brought together in one gigantic refugee camp. The legacy of the Gold Rush and the silver lode will forever mark this city. Its spirit helped to bring San Francisco back from ruin, rising from a barren and burnt landscape to its present glory. What the people of that time found was that the beauty of the city was not in its buildings but in its people, who were bold and brash and creative and crafty. Their strength made its rebuilding possible.

CHAPTER 5
Crime of the Century
LOS ANGELES TIMES BOMBING
- 1910 -

WITH THE RISE OF INDUSTRY IN THE UNITED STATES in the late 1800s, there was also a rise in the organizing of skilled trades workers into unions, notably by the American Federation of Labor (AFL). The battles over union representation were often fierce, and were at times violent.

Los Angeles withstood the onslaught of union organizing well into the twentieth century. Unlike the larger eastern cities, skilled

Firefighters at work after the Los Angeles Times building was bombed.
Courtesy of the California History Room, California State Library, Sacramento

trades workers rather than unskilled factory workers made up a significant portion of the city's population. At the forefront in the fight against unionism were the Los Angeles Merchants and Manufacturers Association (M&M) and the National Erectors Association (NEA). These two organizations, representing many of the businesses in Los Angeles, waged well-funded campaigns to stop union organizing.

At the same time there was a strong surge in support for the Progressive Party in California, a reform movement that was part of a national trend. The Progressives supported women's suffrage; electoral reforms such as referendum, recall, and initiative; and government based on civil service rather than political patronage. A corrupt city government, headed by Democrats, was turned out of office by the Good Government Party (the Goo Goos, as they were known then) in 1909. While this group worked to bring reform to local government, they received little support from the union movement, which had supported the Socialist Party candidate. The M&M and the NEA used labor support of the Socialists to good effect, creating an uneasy alliance with the Goo Goos to curtail local union organizing and promote business.

In the summer of 1910, a concerted effort again was made to organize skilled tradesmen in Los Angeles. The AFL funded experienced organizers from San Francisco and elsewhere who, under the guidance of the Los Angeles Central Labor Council, started to gain a foothold in local industries. Strikes were called, and the fight was on.

The most notable target of this battle was Gen. Harrison Gray Otis, publisher of the *Los Angeles Times,* who had maintained an open shop (one that is not organized for collective bargaining) for more than twenty years. Otis had the dubious distinction of being named by the 1907 AFL convention "the most unfair, unscrupulous, and malignant enemy of organized labor in America."

Otis used his newspaper to attack ferociously; fight him, and he came back even more viciously. The *Times*'s headlines screamed that out-of-town union bosses were trying to create bloodshed. The paper's vitriolic articles caused the unions to sue Otis and his editors for criminal libel. While in San Francisco on business, Otis and his son-in-law, Harry Chandler, were arrested; they were out on bail in a matter of hours.

The *Times* did not let up. The paper accused the unions of assaults on workmen, attempts to blow up buildings, and other attacks to create havoc for open-shop employers. To stop the strikes, the M&M convinced the Los Angeles City Council to outlaw picketing. Soon strikers were being arrested for violating this ordinance, and the strikes collapsed.

As socialist Fred Wheeler saw it: "They promised us a square deal and we got a round club and a square jail from the plunderers that now we know mask behind the control of misnamed good government groups in power and out of power in this city, built by the toil and sweat of the laborer."

Los Angeles was now pitted in what can only be described as a class war: the middle class and employers on one side, and the skilled tradesmen and unskilled workers on the other. Throughout the country violence was part and parcel of the union movement on both sides, and Los Angeles was no exception. The NEA, led by Walter Drew, used this to its advantage by claiming that attacks had been planned. Additionally, the various unions may have been united to fight for the closed shop (one in which an employer hires only union members in good standing), but they often did not get along, with some being more radical than others. This divisiveness also played into the hands of the employers, who pitted one union against another.

Drew and the NEA took on the International Association of Bridge, Structural and Ornamental Iron Workers (IABSOIW), using lies, deceit, physical assault, espionage, and other unscrupulous means to beat back the union's efforts in Los Angeles. Into this fight, as well as others, came labor organizers and strategists, willing to battle Drew's well-funded campaign of union and union-member busting.

James and John Joseph (J.J.) McNamara were brothers by birth and politics. J.J. was the secretary-treasurer of the very same union that Drew was attacking, which had mounted unsuccessful challenges to United States Steel in Pennsylvania and elsewhere. James was a labor activist, although few in the union movement knew him; the two had worked on strike organizing throughout the country. Often, where they organized, physical force and incendiary devices had been used to incite and unite the workers. J.J. sent James to Los Angeles to help in the strikes in any way he could. Angered by the depth and breadth of the employers' strength and the futility of the workers' plight, James once again planned his own extracurricular activities.

With the help of others, James obtained the needed ingredients for his bombs. In his hotel room on the afternoon of September 30, 1910, McNamara created three time bombs. Each clock was attached to a battery that had a wire running to a can filled with nitroglycerin. At about 5:30 P.M., James left his hotel with his packages. The timers were set to go off at about 1:00 A.M., when the number of staff at the Times building was at its lowest. He placed a suitcase next to some barrels in an alley next to the building. Unbeknownst to him, the barrels were filled with ink, a flammable liquid. He then went to the home of H. G. Otis and planted a bomb there. Finally, he left his explosive calling card at the home of Felix Zeehandelaar, the secretary of the M&M. James then left to return to his hotel, where he checked out and headed for the train to San Francisco.

Early in the morning on October 1, 1910, as the night crew of about one hundred worked feverishly to prepare the newspaper for morning publication, an explosion outside the building destroyed the wall of the first floor. Smaller explosions followed, presumably from the igniting of ink barrels. The initial blast was felt blocks away. The building went up in flames almost immediately.

Billowing black smoke consumed the building. Those inside moved away from the explosion if they could, but they were trapped on the upper floors as fire overtook the stairwells. Screaming from windows as the fire rapidly approached, some could not wait any longer and attempted to jump, to either injury or death. When firefighters came bearing nets, several of the editors and pressmen jumped to safety, although at least one jumped and missed the net, dying from the fall. The pressmen on the sixth floor, with the help of a ladder stretched across an alley to the roof of the rooming house next door, narrowly escaped across to the other building; one man using a telegraph wire strung between the two buildings, crossed hand over hand to get away.

It was clear that the building would be a total loss. Those outside who attempted to enter the building were forced away by policemen brandishing their weapons. Finally, as electric wires fell to the ground, the crowd moved back; the building was finally consumed. As a *Times* writer expressed it in a delayed edition that day: "For those in the wreck there was no aid; God only could care for their souls. Human agencies were of no avail."

Otis himself was in Mexico, sent by President William Howard Taft as the U.S. representative at the Centennial of Mexican Independence. Harry Chandler was in charge; he had left just moments before the blast. He returned to find his secretary dead and his father-in-law's paper in ruins. He gathered the survivors and announced that General Otis had planned for such an occurrence. An emergency printing plant was waiting, and the owners of the *Los Angeles Herald,* which Otis also owned, had offered their help. He sent the staff to the College Street location, telling them that they had two hours to have a paper on the street. A one-page newspaper was printed that day. With a headline that read "Unionist Bombs Wreck the Times; Many Seriously Injured," the lead editorial rallied the forces against the unions: "They can kill our men and wreck our buildings, but, by the God above! they cannot kill the *Times.*"

James McNamara was long gone from the scene. Arriving in San Francisco, he learned that his bomb had done much more damage than he had planned. He later stated that he had no intention of killing anyone. Paranoia struck McNamara. Thinking he was being looked for and in danger, he left San Francisco for Seattle, but he felt no safer there. Finally he traveled on to Salt Lake City, where he hid at the home of his brother's Iron Workers Union colleague, J. F. Munsey.

J.J. McNamara worried about his brother's mental state. He sent word to James that he should move on to Nebraska, where their sister and mother were. He sent a friend, Frank Eckhoff, to guide him. Eckhoff found the despondent McNamara ready to take his own life. He convinced James to accompany him to Chicago; from there friends took him to Wisconsin on an extended hunting trip to hide him. Over the next six weeks, James put himself together again. When hunting season ended and he returned to civilization, he was well enough to resume his criminal work.

He joined his brother and other conspirators, and they planned new bombings in Los Angeles for Christmas time. Of the three planned events, only one actually was set, killing the night watchman at Llewellyn Iron Works and causing about $25,000 in damage. The other two, one at Baker Iron Works and one at the Times plant on College Street, were never planted. Ortie McManigal, the man sent by the McNamaras to do the job, claimed that it had been too dangerous to achieve.

According to the book *The People v. Clarence Darrow* by Geoffrey Cowan, James and Ortie set several bombs over the next few months throughout the East and Midwest. It was only a matter of time before they would get caught.

The city of Los Angeles was a mess. The Good Government council and mayor, desperately trying to hold onto office, looked to find the best person to investigate the bombing and bring justice for those who had lost their lives. They turned to William J. Burns, the detective whose company, the Burns Agency, was one of the great investigative companies to lead the search for the perpetrators. Burns was both famous and infamous—a celebrity detective—but he had proven his ability when in 1905 he led the Secret Service team that uncovered criminal fraud in land and timber dealings in Oregon. So, in fighting corporate greed, he had established his credentials with the Progressives throughout the nation. He was also a friend to President Roosevelt and had been written up by none other than the esteemed author Lincoln Steffens, among others.

After Oregon he moved on to San Francisco, where he uncovered graft operations involving the city's leaders and corporate executives. The trials up north had just finished about the time of the bombings in Los Angeles, and Burns was the natural choice to lead the investigation.

Burns had already started to see connections to the McNamara brothers and their cohorts. An iron contractor, McClintic, Marshall and Company, had hired Burns to investigate a bombing of bridge girders. Burns suspected the Iron Workers Union. The L.A. bomb and the McClintic bombs were identically made, with a battery, clock, and a can of nitroglycerin. He agreed to take on the case under the condition that he worked without reporting to anyone until the case was solved.

The choice of Burns angered General Otis and the M&M, mostly because Burns had implicated Otis in the San Francisco graft trials. They hired Earl Rogers, a famous criminal defense lawyer, to run a separate investigation.

Organized labor and its supporters refused to believe that union activists had set the bomb. In fact union investigators had their own theory: They claimed that it had been a natural gas leak that had exploded, not dynamite. And they claimed that the unexploded bombs at Otis and Zeehandelaar were planted to be able to point the finger at unionists instead of at Otis and his failure to fix the leak. "No union man blew up the *Times*," claimed their report. Eugene V. Debs, the popular Socialist Party presidential candidate, even went as far as claiming that antiunion activists had blown up the paper, with the implied accusation that Otis and Drew were behind it all.

Burns worked for months on the case. The mayor finally cut off his source of income due to lack of results. But a reward of $100,000 had been offered by the M&M. Burns borrowed from friends and kept on searching for needed proof.

Finally, on April 22, 1911, J.J. McNamara was detained by Indianapolis police who acted on extradition papers charging him with murder for the bombings at the Los Angeles Times and the Llewellyn Iron Works. Standing in the courtroom in Indianapolis to oversee the shipping of one McNamara brother back to Los Angeles were Burns and Walter Drew of the NEA. They then went with local police to the union's headquarters and ransacked the offices in search of evidence of union complicity.

Unbeknownst to J.J., Burns had abducted his brother and their friend Ortie McManigal, taking them from Michigan to Illinois ten days before. After some persuasive discussions with McManigal, Burns was able to get Ortie to confess to his role and those of the two McNamaras and other coconspirators in the L.A. bombings. All three men were transported back to California in different cars on the same train, each brother unaware that the other was onboard.

The public arrest and extradition of J.J. set unions and their supporters in motion. Not wasting any time, the AFL denounced the arrest. They immediately called on their legal eagle, the great Clarence Darrow, to defend J.J., and, when later informed, James as well.

It was an easy decision for the union. Clarence Darrow was one of the most famous criminal defense attorneys in the United States and a longtime union supporter. Among his victories for the unions was the infamous trial of Big Bill Haywood and others for murder in Idaho four years before. The similarities were obvious: a major union fight in Idaho, the union organizers pursued by Pinkertons, abducted back to Idaho at gunpoint, only to be found not guilty. Suspicion of both the employers and the detective agency was easily transferred to Los Angeles M&M, the NEA, and the Burns Detective Agency. Surely the charges were trumped up, because the Haywood case proved that the capitalists were capable of using their money and influence to discredit unionism, even if it were through the creation of false charges.

Darrow had been in semiretirement, doing corporate work that was relatively easy after serious illness had threatened his life a few years earlier. But he saw in this case the kind of story of industrial injustice that made his blood flow. He could not resist; he took the case.

He made it clear to union leaders that they would have to plan and execute a crusade that would move the people's minds away from the twenty dead men to the injustice of blaming the McNamaras, victims of capitalists and symbols of a united union movement. He had to use the Idaho case to cast each of the players in this case into the proper light: the McNamaras as victims of overzealous detectives, an informer who gave in to threats of harm to himself or his family and gave false statements, and employers greedy enough to use the deaths of their employees to keep from paying decent wages. And the union movement had to stand as one in support of this scenario. Within days everyone was on board; the movement stood united behind the McNamaras. They had been framed.

Los Angeles was also at this time in the throes of a fierce municipal election battle. The unions, dissatisfied with the Good Government mayor and city council, threw their support to the Socialist Party candidate, Job Harriman, who was running for mayor. In an upset Harriman won the Democratic primary, setting himself up to win the November election.

Even the arrests of the McNamaras and McManigal did not lessen the optimism felt by political progressives that Los Angeles would soon be run by Socialists. (But, it should be pointed out, it would not be the first time Socialists won local elections. Several towns and cities had elected Socialist Party candidates.) Darrow would prove that the boys were framed, and the employers of Los Angeles would take a beating. If there were worries, it was that by the time of the election, women would have the right to vote in California, and reaching this considerable number of new voters would be a tremendous challenge.

The Socialists ran a moderate campaign of reform in government, business and industry, and other areas. It was not particularly radical, although its call for municipalization of utilities such as water and gas was meant to broaden the party's appeal. Workers voted Socialist; the middle class and businessmen did not. But workers were in the midst of a series of strikes throughout the city, and the Good Government Party had been the one that had passed the draconian antipicketing ordinance. The resentment of moneyed interests was great. With more workers than employers, the Socialist victory, first in the Democratic primary, and then, barring unforeseen defections, in the general election seemed assured.

The nation's eyes were on Los Angeles. Moderates and radicals were working together throughout the country to support the McNamaras; even the radical Industrial Workers of the World (IWW) stood next to the American Federation of Labor on this issue.

The propaganda machine was running at full speed. The Socialists played up the fact that the Good Government mayor and council had joined in the conspiracy against the McNamaras, because it had been their report that determined that dynamite had been used, and they had hired William Burns who abducted the brothers and brought them back to California for trial. Beaten on the streets and thrown into jail for being union members, picketers saw the parallel between their fate and those unfairly charged with arson and murder. The issue was "who controlled the police power?"

Even the American Federation of Labor's Samuel Gompers, an avowed anti-Socialist, endorsed Harriman's candidacy. What could go wrong so late in the campaign?

Everything. The trial was set for October, and the municipal elections for December.

The right wing coalesced, bringing together Progressives, Democrats and Republicans, church groups, various business associations, and other middle-class organizations. Sides had been chosen; clear lines determined whom each voter would support. The class war had moved to an all-out fight at the ballot box.

Voter registration ended on November 9, 1911. The new women voters totaled almost 75,000 to the men's 100,000. But the split of support by precinct put two-thirds of the women in precincts that supported Good Government candidates. It would be a close election. Harriman, who had been the clear favorite over incumbent George Alexander before the female electorate had joined in, now was finding he was in real race to the finish.

Clarence Darrow was in a dilemma. From the beginning he had believed his clients guilty. Yet he had taken the case nevertheless, and he was determined to make a go of it. He put together a politically correct defense team: Socialist Job Harriman, a moderate business-friendly president of the Los Angeles school board, a judge, and another criminal lawyer of note.

And while the court of public opinion was clearly on the defendants' side, the legal case was somewhat stickier, and the politics of the courthouse unlike any he had faced before. The moneyed interests of Los Angeles had controlled the courts for a very long time, and the Good Government reformers had not yet made progress in breaking the bond between business interests and judges.

The well-funded prosecution also was daunting. Darrow pleaded with the AFL to increase funding over the original amount they had promised, allowing him to hire more detectives and experts.

Gompers agreed to increase the amount locals needed to raise to cover the expenses.

Unlike the Pinkerton-Haywood case in Idaho, Darrow saw, as the case proceeded through preliminary stages, that Burns had developed solid evidence against James: similarities of explosive devices used; identification of James as "Jim Brice" who had stayed at the hotel and had been overheard planning the conspiracy; and an ironclad confession and testimony from one of the conspirators. But the case against J.J. was weaker. Certainly J.J. knew what his brother was capable of doing when he sent him to Los Angeles. But establishing his link to the conspiracy before the fact was the prosecutor's headache. Yet J.J. was vulnerable on the Llewellyn Iron Works bombing, in which he helped plan the action.

Darrow was not above the very same tactics of influence, fabrication, and bribery that he accused his opponents of using. He hired Larry Sullivan, a former boxer and investigator, to hound prosecution witnesses, intimidating them into not testifying. Another investigator offered $5,000 to the key eyewitness to the conspiracy if she would leave the state for the duration of the trial. A detective was sent to convince an out-of-state witness not to return to California to testify. Darrow even attempted to make an important member of Burns's own staff into a double agent.

The promised AFL financial support was not coming in as quickly as expected. By the end of August, only about $80,000 had been collected, significantly under the $200,000 Darrow had demanded when he took the case. And what money had been raised was just about gone.

With the trial approaching, Darrow was anxious. He hired Bert Franklin, a detective, to research the jury pool, developing information that would help him choose a good jury. But Franklin went a step further; he visited the home of one potential juror, Robert Bain, and offered a bribe for his vote of acquittal. Bain accepted the bribe.

The trial was to begin on October 11, 1911. But the selection of the jury took almost two months. During that time, of course, Socialist Job Harriman had won the Democratic primary for mayor. Women registered to vote in droves. And Clarence Darrow attempted to keep damaging evidence concerning J.J. McNamara that had been taken from the Indianapolis headquarters of the Iron Workers union from being used in California.

Over the next seven weeks, James McNamara took a beating, and J.J.'s innocent facade began to slip. It became increasingly obvious that James was guilty. Each time Darrow attempted to present a defense, he seemed to make things worse. Friends suggested alternative defenses, from "necessity" (this is a war between capital and workers, and McNamara was justified in acting in any way necessary to secure better wages and working conditions) to "insanity" caused by the oppression of the industrial system. The first was similar to John Brown's defense of his attack on Harpers Ferry, Virginia, before the Civil War. The second was a way to bring into testimony and evidence the conditions of the workers that drove men to bombing. But neither defense was acceptable to Darrow.

Others urged him to plead the men guilty, admitting that their actions were wrong. But Darrow realized that he had a problem there: The McNamaras were not his clients; the American Federation of Labor, the organization that had hired him, was. And he had to protect his client. A guilty plea would not be acceptable to the AFL after the staunch position, effort, and fund-raising that the unions had done in their defense. After all, the AFL was antiviolence, a conservative position in the face of the IWW's radicalism and the Socialist Party's pragmatism.

At the beginning of November, Lincoln Steffens, the muckraking writer who had himself written about Clarence Darrow in earlier years, came to Los Angeles to observe and write about the trial. Steffens fancied himself a dealmaker as well as a muckraker. But he came with the expressed purpose of writing the truth about the trial and the union's involvement in this class war. He believed that J.J. McNamara and his brother were fighters in a war, and as such they should not be tried for murder; they should be treated as prisoners of war. When the war ended, they would be set free. He wanted to write a series of articles that explored the fight between labor and capital; he wanted to expose the war so that there could be a peace.

After a couple of weeks of interviewing all of the various participants, Steffens suggested that Darrow accompany him to the San Diego estate of E. W. Scripps, the owner of the United Press and several working-class papers. Darrow was almost despondent about the fate of the McNamaras. On the train back to Los Angeles, Steffens offered a possible solution: plead the men guilty; J.J. would not do prison time, and James would take whatever the court doled out, short of hanging.

Darrow agreed because J.J.'s going free was the focus of the union's involvement. The AFL did not know James and did not care about his fate, except as far as it affected his brother's freedom. But Darrow demanded that the *Times* ownership agree to this settlement, and that he in no way could be seen as having knowledge of the settlement before the prosecution did.

Steffens set out to broker the deal, visiting a friend of Harry Chandler, who took the proposal to the owners of the *Times*. What Darrow understood was that the only reason the opposition would buy this deal was that it would undermine Job Harriman's, and the Socialist Party's, municipal election campaign. Labor would look as if it were culpable, and the Good Government candidates would gain the higher moral ground. This change in perception would bring about defeat of the Socialists in the December 5 election.

In the end Chandler, Drew, and Otis didn't care if justice was done so much as they cared about the water aqueduct being built to bring stolen Owens Valley water to Los Angeles. They cared about having enough water so they could subdivide the land they had bought in the San Fernando Valley for a pittance and sell it at an enormous profit. And they cared that Los Angeles remain an open-shop town so that they could run it without interference from the workers and their unions. Chandler liked the settlement as long as the announcement was made no later than December 1.

But the stumbling block became getting the agreement of District Attorney John Fredericks. Negotiations were being handled by intermediaries, and misinterpretations of the meaning of the offer played a pivotal role in the failure to come to terms. Fredericks wanted to convict both men; he did not care about whether one hanged or not. Darrow needed J.J. to go free and James to stay alive. Meanwhile, Walter Drew was amenable to J.J. going free as long as James pled guilty and helped convict other members of the Iron and Structural Workers Union's executive committee. And each of the brothers offered himself up onto the mantle of justice if the other brother were spared punishment.

Fredericks, however, knew of Franklin's bribe of Robert Bain, and he knew that Franklin had attempted to bribe another juror, George Lockwood, who had reported the attempt to him. Bain was on the jury and a sure vote for acquittal. Fredericks decided to use procedural rules to choose two more jurors as alternates; then, at the appropriate time, he would expose Bain. He was overjoyed when Lockwood's name was called for empanelling, because Lockwood had been approached again by Franklin.

The trap was ready to ensnare the defense in legal sin. Franklin met Lockwood to make the deal, but so did the Los Angeles Police Department. Darrow himself walked into the trap unknowingly when he showed up serendipitously at the scene just before the arrest was made.

Franklin's arrest was front-page news. It threw a monkey wrench into the defense's public relations, and it changed the political and legal climate. Now more than ever Darrow wanted a settlement. The DA had not told the press that Darrow had been at the scene of the bribe, and Darrow was wary of the DA's benevolence. Time was running out.

Thursday, November 30, was Thanksgiving Day. While there was no court session, Darrow knew he had until Friday's deadline to get a settlement. He spent the day with the McNamaras in the jail, trying to convince them to plead guilty. He and his legal team met separately with each man. Then, after Thanksgiving dinner, they met with the two men together. Jim made it clear that he would plead to murder if it would free J.J. And J.J. said no—he would plead to the Llewellyn Iron Works bombing if James's life were saved. James said no.

The lawyers left and sent for Father Edward Brady, a Catholic priest, to spend time with James. When they returned to the jail, James was more amenable. In the end he allowed his brother to plead, reportedly, for the sake of his friends in the labor movement.

Everyone involved in the case knew that the deal had been made, except for one man—Job Harriman. Darrow decided to keep him in the dark to spare him the choice of supporting his client or supporting his party. Labor's representative was Ed Knockles. When told by Darrow that night of the decision, Knockles first fought it. The AFL had just finished meeting at its annual convention in Atlanta and had passed resolutions supporting the innocence of these two men. But soon Knockles came to realize the futility of the situation and he, too, agreed.

Fredericks went to see General Otis. The old publisher spit fire at him, demanding that both hang. But he came around eventually. After a visit by Darrow and Fredericks with the judge, the stage was set.

The next day, the climax unfolded. In a surprise to the crowd, J. J. McNamara came into the courtroom. He had not been there since the first day, since the trial on the bombing of the L.A. Times building involved James. Next, each defendant withdrew his original plea and admitted his guilt. The trial of the century was over.

James was quoted as saying, "Well, if I swing, I'll swing for a principle." He was sentenced to life in prison on December 5. J.J. received fifteen years.

Working-class Los Angeles was in shock. Men and women wept openly, then became angry, accusing the McNamaras of selling out. Job Harriman knew his campaign was lost; thousands would desert him now that he had supported the innocence of two guilty men.

National labor leaders felt betrayed. They had thrown themselves totally into the fray on the side of the McNamaras. They had had no warning of the deal, no opportunity to protect themselves. Darrow, however, dismissed the idea that the decision was a defeat for labor. He said that this was one event in the inevitable growth of the labor movement. There were more victories to be had up ahead; in time the forces of oppression would be defeated.

Thirty-eight others were arraigned in Indianapolis in 1912, an outgrowth of this trial. They stood trial and, based on the testimony of Ortie McManigal, were found guilty of a bombing conspiracy, convincing many that unions and their leaders were lawless. But also as a result of this trial, the federal Commission on Industrial Relations issued a report detailing the terrible conditions created by employers that led to the use of violence by some union workers.

Job Harriman was defeated by the incumbent mayor on December 5, 1911. Whether he lost due to the confessions or because of the infusion of the women's vote is still a matter for debate.

Without a Socialist Party victory, Los Angeles had been turned over to the "expansionists." The aqueduct being built to bring water to the area took another two years to complete. With it the San Fernando Valley was subdivided and paved. Because of that aqueduct, hundreds of people would die when a dam built to hold the stolen water collapsed in 1928.

Los Angeles labor unions never really recovered from the setbacks of that trial. Los Angeles remained a city favorable to employers until the New Deal legitimized union organizing, more than thirty years later. And the reelected government failed to tame the police department, and for many years the police acted as the oppressor-arm of capital.

Clarence Darrow himself stood trial for the attempted bribery of George Lockwood the next year in Los Angeles. Although he was found not guilty, his reputation was tarnished as a result. In 1913 he was again on trial for bribery of Robert Bain. The jury came back hung, 8–4, for conviction. But by that time John Fredericks had his eye on the governorship, and though he did indict Darrow again, he did not pursue the case. He was elected governor the next year.

Darrow left Los Angeles after agreeing to a deal in which he promised never to return to the city. Eventually he moved out from under the shadow of the case to even greater prominence; he died in 1938, at the age of eighty, a well-respected man. James McNamara became the darling of the newly rising Communist movement. He died in prison, as did two others who had aided him in Los Angeles. J.J. served most of his sentence, being released in 1922; he returned to union work but eventually was expelled for stealing. James died two months before his brother in 1941.

General Otis died in 1917, and Harry Chandler took over the *Los Angeles Times*. Los Angeles itself grew beyond its boundaries, becoming a megalopolis. Many industries developed around Southern California, and unions organized their workers. Strikes were called; some were won, and some were lost. And the trial of the century, and what brought it about, has slipped into the vagaries of historical memory.

CHAPTER 6

Fire in the Hole

ARGONAUT MINE DISASTER
- 1922 -

IF YOU WERE TO DRIVE EAST OUT OF SACRAMENTO ON State Route 16 and then head south on Highway 49, you would find yourself in the heart of the Mother Lode, California's gold country. The road winds into the foothills of the Sierra Nevada Mountains, and pretty soon you would arrive in Jackson, a small town that was once the "Mecca of the Mother Lode."

When gold was first discovered at Sutter's Mill in Sacramento in 1849, the miners who rushed to the area spread out in their search for

The Argonaut Mine as it appeared in 1947. Special Collections, General Library, University of California–Davis

riches. As they moved south and east into the Sierra Nevada mountain range, surface mining and panning riverbeds was the quickest and easiest way to find gold. The town of Jackson was established when some of the gold miners realized that there was money to be made by supplying miners with necessities for their work, from food to tents, equipment, and clothing. Eventually the easily reached gold panned out, but Jackson continued on when hard-rock mining began about a mile out of town.

Several hard-rock mines came and went in the Jackson area during the late 1800s, but two survived well into the twentieth century: the Kennedy mine and its neighboring rival, the Argonaut. In these mines workers dug deep, nearly a mile deep, to find and extract the low-grade gold ore. The holes that were made had to be shored up with strong timber or else the earth was likely to claim back the newly made void, collapsing the sides of the rock walls to refill the hole from which the rock had been taken. The work was excruciatingly hard, the hours monotonously long, the pay infinitesimally small—up to $4.00 a day. The dangers to life and limb were enormous. And one night in August of 1922, the dangers took their toll upon a group of unsuspecting miners, deep down in the Argonaut mine.

At the Argonaut, there was a three-compartment shaft that allowed the ore to be removed for processing; water pipes, electricity, and telephony wires to be laid down to the mining levels; and the miners to come and go. The shaft was cut on an angle rather than on the vertical, so the two skips that moved men, equipment, and ore ran on tracks, pulled up and released downward by sturdy cable from a hoist station on the surface. Since electric lighting was limited to the shaft itself, miners wore hats with small lamps that burned carbide (a carbon compound that glowed when ignited) that attached to their hats to give them light in the dark passageways.

Ventilation was provided by way of the shaft of the neighboring defunct Muldoon mine, on top of which was a huge and powerful fan

Hard-Rock Gold Mining

When the gold is in the rock and the rock is below the ground, extraction is costly and increasingly dangerous. It is estimated that the Argonaut's take from a ton of rock was about three ounces of pure gold. With the government setting the price of gold at $22 per ounce, that meant that the owners of the mine received $66 for the efforts of their miners.

First the vein must be found, so blasting and digging downward into the rock must be done until rock with gold in it was found. Although sometimes there was a high-quality vein of gold and large chunks of gold could be broken away from the rock, often the percentage of gold in the rock was so small that it wasn't worth mining unless you had the right equipment and processes to extract the gold from the rock. The rock was blown with dynamite, and the pieces of gold ore (more like specks of gold in rock) were collected, smashed into smaller, more manageable pieces, and then hoisted to the surface in skips—large bucket-shaped cars that could hold as much as four tons—for further chemical extraction. The vein of gold ore was followed horizontally and vertically until it ran out; the downward blasting and digging proceeded until another level—or drift—with enough gold ore to be mined was found, and the process of blasting, smashing, and removing ore resumed. Drifts were then connected through raises—mining of rock upward on an angle—that allowed the men to move from one drift to another.

that drew out the air from deep in the Argonaut. Without that fan the contaminated air would make it impossible to breathe, let alone work. The Muldoon also provided a second exit from the mine as required by federal and state regulations.

Though few had been born in the United States, the miners were mostly European immigrants from Spain, Italy, and the Baltics. Immigrant miners often saved their meager earnings and sent them home to bring other relatives to the United States.

Ordinarily about seventy-five men worked eight-hour shifts in the mines, which ran twenty-four hours a day, every day of the year. On Sundays the shifts were smaller, fewer than fifty most times, because men often took this day to visit family or to vacation. On this Sunday night, August 27, 1922, there were forty-seven lunch pails, one for each man in the mine. Forty-seven down below, blasting holes, breaking rock, clearing ore. Little did these forty-seven miners know that a fire had broken out above them, at the 3,000-foot drift, and that they were in danger.

To guard against potential theft of gold ore, the men came to work in street clothes, which they removed in one room; naked, they walked into another room where they donned miner's clothes and left their lunch pails before heading for a skip to take them to the drift, or level, where they would be mining. The pails were delivered to the miners while they were down below, then picked up after the lunch break and returned to the changing rooms empty. At the end of the shift, the men returned to the changing rooms, reversing their steps and actions. In that way, no one—at least management hoped—was able to hide valuable ore successfully.

The Argonaut mine sat about a mile out of Jackson, a little higher up a hill than its neighbor, the Kennedy. The two had been fighting for years over a myriad of issues, but mostly it was about the trespass of the Kennedy into gold-bearing veins that were on Argonaut land. Both mines were "wet" mines—nearly 75,000 gallons of water were used in a twenty-four-hour period (and remember, the mines were open every day of the year). Both mines were exhaustingly hot, the temperature rising a degree for every 100-foot drop; that meant that a 40-degree day outside would be an 89-degree work area at 4,900 feet. In California, 40-degree days were more the exception than the rule, so temperatures often went past the century mark. Miners came out of the mines soaked, and they left their mining clothes hanging on a rack in the changing rooms to dry in time for their next shifts.

Owned by a group of absentee investors, the Argonaut was run by Superintendent Virgilio S. Garbarini, considered one of the mining geniuses of the West. A self-taught engineer, he had risen in rank from miner to become a consultant to several mines. Garbarini went to work at the Argonaut in 1909, where, as master mechanic, he had designed the tramway and cable system that ran the enormous, bucket-shaped skips up and down the shaft. He also designed the ventilation system used at the Argonaut. He was also politically powerful, having served as mayor of Jackson. The respect he garnered meant that his decisions were not questioned often.

However, night shifts were run by the shift bosses, who made all the decisions that were ordinarily made by management during the day. When an emergency arose, the shift boss would call the manager. On this night Clarence Bradshaw was the shift boss; the manager was Benjamin Sanguinetti. Their decisions, as well as the decisions of Garbarini and the miners themselves, would determine the fate of the forty-seven trapped miners.

Bradshaw was responsible for taking the lunch buckets down to the men below. Piling them in a skip, he stopped at various levels to distribute them, finally staying at the 4,650 level to eat with some of the miners. With two others he headed back up the shaft. As the skip rose, the smell of smoke began to fill the shaft, and the smoke blocked Bradshaw and the others from seeing what lay above. Finally the skip sailed past the fire itself and escaped to the fresh air above. The fire was along the ceiling of the shaft and was pulled downward, drawn— as was the smoke—by the exhaust fan in the old Muldoon shaft. The fire itself was in the manway, the compartment with the electrical and telephone wires that also acted as a climbing passageway for miners heading up and down short distances within the mine. But the other two passageways were threatened, and they would not be usable at all if the fire was not stopped quickly.

The first the miners below knew of the fire was likely to have been when they noticed that the lunch buckets had yet to be picked up. Ordinarily, the mine rats would have been scurrying around and over the pails in search of the smallest crumbs. But on this night the rats were not there, and that would have tipped the miners to something unnatural occurring elsewhere in the mine. A call to the surface confirmed their suspicions. Told that there was a fire in the shaft, the second part of the message told them they were on their own, "and we are going to try to put it out." No rescue attempt was going to be made; they needed to act quickly to protect themselves.

The men turned to Ernie Miller, who was the only one among them to have survived a similar situation. Ernie had been in another mine, Granite Mountain, when there was a fire that took 120 lives, but he and others had survived fifteen days behind a bulkhead that kept the bad air out until they were rescued. Could he do that again?

Gathering the men he could find, Miller moved them up to the 4,600 drift to reach the Muldoon shaft, but the air there had already become so contaminated that they had to turn back. They eventually made it up to the 4,350 drift, where they finally decided to make a stand. Picking up every piece of debris they could find, they brought it all to a crosscut where they built a wall, but smoke started to permeate the barrier. Taking most of their clothing off and tearing them into shreds, the miners dipped the cloth strips in mud and filled the holes. Then they started building a second bulkhead about 25 feet behind the first.

Meanwhile, Bradshaw and Sanguinetti and others were attempting to put out the fire in the shaft but to no avail, due primarily to the fact that the burning timbers were near the roof of the shaft. That meant that to quench the fire, the water had to go up, but gravity forced it down to the floor of the shaft. So, when they emptied a water holding tank 1,000 feet above the fire, the water did not have enough pressure to reach the fire itself.

When Garbarini arrived at the hoist station, a suggestion was made to reverse the Muldoon fan's direction or to stop it completely to keep the men from being suffocated. Whatever you do, he ordered, do not stop the fan or reverse it. The fan would take hours to stop and reverse, and, not knowing what the miners were doing below, doing so might actually make it more difficult for the trapped men to breathe.

Garbarini also agreed that the main focus should be on putting out the fire, not saving the men below. Whether this was a decision to protect the investment of the owners or a logical decision based on where the fire was and the dangers of sending the skips down not knowing for certain on which level the men would be (telephone communications, along with electricity, had been severed at the 3,000-foot drift as the result of fire damage) is hard to say.

Early in the morning of August 28, government officials and the press were informed. Emergency teams and the press corps came from other parts of the state to a disaster that would gain international notoriety. By dawn the townspeople had heard and were congregating at the mine. The vigil had begun.

A working committee was established that made decisions and controlled information going out to the press. The committee decided that the only way to rescue the miners was to dig into the mine from the rival Kennedy mine. The Kennedy and the Argonaut had been connected at various points in their contentious relationship before being closed off completely after a fire in the Argonaut in 1919. The ends of certain Kennedy drifts were as close as 5 feet from drifts of the Argonaut, although those that close were not viable entryways to pursue opening.

Because the Kennedy was situated below the opening of the Argonaut's shaft and had a vertical shaft, its depth was dramatically shorter than that of the Argonaut. With the Kennedy management's blessing and help, miners began to cut through the rock at the 3,600-foot level and later at the 3,900-foot drift, which mirrored the 4,200 and 4,500 levels in the damaged mine. When this approach was presented to the committee, one of the members stated firmly that it would take two to three weeks to break through at those levels. Another proposed to turn off the Muldoon fan and send men in to open closed ventilation doors, forcing out the bad air and locating the miners in a matter of a day. But Garbarini's reputation and political clout shot down the idea. Other plans were proposed but discarded. Without another viable choice, the digging began.

The rescue crew of miners faced obstacle after obstacle in their attempts to break through to the Argonaut. In the previous fire both mines had been flooded to stop the flames, so there was the problem of mud and debris that had collected. Then the timbers that had been holding the roof of the drift open had fallen and rotted. These had to be removed and replaced to protect the rescue crew. And then 60 feet of solid stone had to be removed to reach the Argonaut side.

Meanwhile, on the Argonaut side, firefighters were trying to put out the fire, which now had engulfed the passageway's three compartments and had burned almost up to the 2,500 station. Wearing a complicated and bulky precursor to SCUBA equipment, firefighters moved a canvas hose 200 feet long down the manway to attach to a special pressurized pipe, so that the water finally was streamed directly onto the fire without stopping. Once the fire on the upper levels was out, workers could build a bulkhead, shutting off the shaft and the fire's inexhaustible supply of oxygen until the flames were extinguished.

The breakthrough from the Kennedy to the Argonaut did indeed take twenty-one days, working around the clock. To the population of miners and their families, it had become obvious that this was no longer a rescue but a recovery. It would have been a miracle had even one person survived after that amount of time. But preparations for rescue continued right to the very end.

The rescuers broke through the first bulkhead, only to find a second one. They knew now that the men were behind that second bulkhead, and they could only hope for the best. In the darkness of the drift, however, it took them some time to finally realize the outcome: The second bulkhead was unfinished at the top. The bad air had not been contained; the miners had to be dead.

The sights and smells of death behind that bulkhead were overwhelming. The first problem facing the recovery team now was that the bodies had decomposed. In an ordinary situation a decomposed body stays relatively intact because the deceased's clothing holds the body together. But the miners had used most of their clothing to patch the walls of the barriers, so the naked bodies had little or no form, making identification that much more difficult.

Eventually, however, preliminary identifications were made. Those who were recognizable were named. Most of the miners had been able to hold onto the brass tokens that identified them on the payroll. And others had wedding rings or some personal object to help in identification. The process of recovery, removal, and preservation went well, except that in the end only forty-six bodies were found inside the drift and its crosscuts. Where was the final body, and who was he?

And then there was the message in the rock. Toward the very back of the drift, a miner lay with a carbide lamp in his hand. Above his body, burned into the rock, was the following message: "3 o/clock gas getting strong"; "Fessel;" "3^{20}"; "4 o/clock." (Later when a photographer brought his equipment down to photograph the rock, the bright lights he used uncovered more words etched into the rock by hand: "3^{15}, half knocked out" and "3^{35}.") The last three letters were written in a downward pattern as the writer himself succumbed to the effects of carbon monoxide and smoke fumes. And he seemed to have signed his name: "Fessel." But the token the body under the message carried was not that of William Fessel but that of a miner whom company officials refused to identify specifically. So where was William Fessel?

Most important to the families waiting above was that the message meant that the men had not suffered greatly, their falling prey to the noxious and toxic air had been relatively quick, and they had gone into a sleep state within a few hours of discovery of the fire, to die a silent, painless death. While the living had suffered through over three weeks of waiting and through hopes dashed by the recovery—a sorrow some would carry to their own graves—the deadly trap had not been a painful one.

In the process of burning the remaining clothing, putrefied from the decay of the dead who wore them, a worker noticed something shiny in the pyre. The worker found a signet ring with the initials "JSN," letters that did not match the initials of any of the miners trapped in the mine. And a further mystery that was never solved was that, when the clothing in the changing room was matched to the bodies of the deceased miners, a forty-eighth set of clothes was found. But the payroll sheet for the day clearly showed only forty-seven workers. This set of clothing was never identified; no one ever claimed the items, and no one, besides William Fessel, the forty-seventh miner, was ever declared missing.

Forty-seven caskets were buried on Friday, September 22, in three separate ceremonies at the Catholic, Protestant, and Greek Orthodox cemeteries. One box was empty, a tribute to William Fessel who, it was hoped, would eventually be found below the water line at the 4,500-foot level.

With the end of the search and the burial of the dead miners, inquisitions began into the cause of the fire and decision making by those responsible. Some intimated that the International Workers of the World (IWW), a radical organization who had organized miners throughout the West, had set the fire. But the IWW had been destroyed by the U.S. government during World War I and had not come back into existence as a viable union afterward. Others tried to make connections between the legal fights the Argonaut was having with the Kennedy in the courts. But nothing was ever determined; it might just have been a spark from the electrical wiring in the manway that lighted a timber.

And while the Argonaut and the Kennedy management made some changes to the way the mines were run, nothing substantive ever came from the investigations. The federal government's focus was on coal mining, and the state's interest in gold and other mineral mines was to keep them producing for as long as they could. In fact no legislation to improve worker safety was passed and implemented during the life of either of these mines, which ended their operations in 1942. Both mines had other fires, but with less damage than in 1922.

The Argonaut mine did not reopen until the fall of 1923. But in the process of "dewatering" the lower levels that had been flooded in the firefighting period, a human corpse was found. And although no one could definitively recognize or identify the dead man, all agreed that it had to be William Fessel. He, too, was laid to rest next to his fellow miners on the hill above Jackson.

The remains of St. Francis Dam. Charles H. Lee Papers, Water Resources Center Archives—University of California, Berkeley

CHAPTER 7

Mulholland's Dam Falls

ST. FRANCIS RESERVOIR FLOOD
- 1928 -

THE EARTH SHOOK, LIKE THERE WAS A MIGHTY earthquake, but that wasn't the half of it. Then there was the sound— a rumbling sound—like no other: a bit like a tornado, a bit like a train coming through . . . but there were no tornadoes back in the mountains, and there were no train tracks nearby. Then there was the smell of dirt and grass and forest and water. That was when it became clear that the dam had crumbled against the force of so much water, and the water was moving down a narrow creek toward a normally peaceful river to take houses, barns, livestock, and people with it.

William Mulholland had a serious problem. As superintendent of Los Angeles Water and Power (LAWP), he had masterminded the taking of the water from the Owens Valley in eastern California for use in the burgeoning development of the small city of Los Angeles. It was a vision he shared with L.A.'s elite—bankers, developers, landowners—who dreamed an idea so fantastic that few believed it ever possible: a green metropolis on southern California desert land. While few in California could ever dream it, the first to feel the devastating effects of this dream were the ranchers and farmers of the Owens Valley, 250 miles away.

The plan was simple: Have someone buy up the land in the Owens Valley, and then sell the land or option the water rights to LAWP. By the time the locals learned about the arrangement, digging would have started on the aqueduct to take the water to Los Angeles. And so it went, and with it went the only hope of the irrigation water the farmers and ranchers of Inyo County needed. The land lost what water had been coming, because not only did Los Angeles take the surface water, LAWP also started to pump the groundwater, emptying the water table and leaving the land without sustenance.

The locals fought in the courts and lost. And then some took the war to the aqueduct itself, blowing up portions to prevent what they clearly saw as water theft. So Mulholland faced the problem of intermittent decreases and stoppages of water flow to his thirsty city.

Mulholland's answer to his problem was to find somewhere to store as much of the water as he could—a year's supply at a minimum—in a safe place within Los Angeles County, deep in the backwoods in the northern part of the county. He chose to build that dam on the San Francisquito Creek, a tributary of the Santa Clara River, which ran through Los Angeles County and into Ventura County, bringing needed water to farms and towns on its way to the Pacific Ocean.

Ventura County residents had been vigilant in protecting their

The Dam Movie

While not named the St. Francis, the building of the dam that led to this disaster was the backdrop for the story in the 1974 film *Chinatown*, directed by Roman Polanski from a Robert Towne screenplay. Detective Jake Gittes is on the trail of a missing teen whose mother, Evelyn Mulwray, is the estranged daughter of Noah Cross, the man who brought Los Angeles its water, and the wife of Hollis Mulwray, chief engineer for the water company. While investigating the disappearance, Gittes stumbles onto the knowledge that large amounts of water are being purposely released into the ocean while there is a drive to build a new dam. In the film Chief Engineer Mulwray publicly states that he is against the construction of this dam because it isn't properly designed and its geography is questionable. Gittes finds that land outside Los Angeles County is being bought up and the water rights taken.

Gittes goes to see Noah Cross, a mighty wealthy man, who is the mastermind behind these maneuvers. At Cross' yacht club, they converse about his daughter and granddaughter. Finally, Gittes, not really understanding why Cross and his friends were buying up the land and pushing for a dam that wasn't needed, asks the obvious questions: If you are so wealthy already, why do you need more? What else is there to buy? Cross answers with some delight, "The future, Mr. Gittes. The future."

In this scene, Towne gives us a picture of the drive of Californians that is central to the understanding of this disaster and many of the other stories in this book. The state was first populated by those who thought they could make it rich on freely flowing rivers of gold. The belief in California, certainly at that time, was that anything is possible, that anything goes. Men like Cross are not satisfied to be wealthy; in fact, they can never be satisfied at all.

water supply after the Owens Valley theft. They fought with Los Angeles to keep the neighboring county from pulling the same stunt on their turf. But their diligence was too narrowly focused, because Mulholland did the paperwork, filed the forms, and held the hearings in Los Angeles to get permission to build the St. Francis Dam without the citizens of Ventura County even noticing.

So it was with some surprise that word began to trickle into the Santa Paula area, 50 miles downstream from the construction site, that the dam was being built. By that time it was too late to stop it. But Los Angeles claimed that none of the water stored would be taken from the Santa Clara River. In fact the plan was to put into the Santa Clara all of the spillover, the excess water brought from the Owens Valley that the dam could not hold. Little did they know how much spillover they might be getting.

The dam was built between two outcroppings or abutments, and while the eastern outcropping was never in question, the western end's shale facing was of some concern to the engineers at LAWP. But it was built anyway, and, even before it was finished, filling began. Fresh, clean Owens Valley water was diverted from the L.A. Aqueduct to be stored behind the St. Francis Dam in a new reservoir.

To Mulholland, the dam, 250 miles away from the battleground from which the water had been taken, would allow him to breathe more easily should his main water supply be cut off again. In addition the water was diverted through two powerhouses that were placed about 3 miles apart to generate power that was then sent via Southern California Edison's wires to light Los Angeles and points south.

While no one could have predicted the disaster that would occur, there were ominous incidents that came to light later during the investigations into the disaster. One such incident happened on the Saturday before the dam's collapse. During a conversation between a local, William Hoke, and the damkeeper, Tony Harnischfeger, Hoke arranged a fishing trip for Wednesday, March 13. The damkeeper replied, "OK, if she [the dam] is still here on Wednesday, why I will come down, and we will go out then." Harnischfeger was concerned about the west abutment.

Signs of leakage were noted by passersby the Saturday before the dam burst. Hoke himself testified later to having seen two streams of water running from the base of the dam. A few days later, he saw a third—this one muddy, a sign of possible leakage in the foundation itself.

The morning before the collapse, Harnischfeger noticed that the dam was leaking. He notified his superiors, who told Mulholland, who drove up to the dam to inspect the leak. Seemingly satisfied that the dam was not in any immediate danger, Mulholland left and returned to Los Angeles, not informing anyone as to his findings. Yet even if he had known the dam was overstressed, there would have been nothing he could have done to stop it from bursting. But could he have warned the towns and farmers and ranchers of the imminent dangers they were facing? Could he have saved the lives of the 400 residents who died later that night?

The first warning residents near the dam had of a problem was the rumble under foot and the roar in the air just before midnight on March 12. Californians are not easily scared by tremors, having experienced any number of tectonic movements in their lifetimes. But the thunderous noise—described by those from the Midwest as sounding like a tornado—sent shivers down their spines. And for some the smell of floodwater was distinct. But by then there was no time to escape, no time to gather their loved ones or protect their livestock or warn their neighbors downstream. There was only time to face the wall of water that swept them, their houses, and their livelihoods into the swell of the 180-foot-high rush of water, concrete, and natural debris.

The water moved at first at an estimated rate of 18 miles per hour down the canyon; when the canyon walls narrowed, the water wall squeezed through, the increased pressure being released upon the unsuspecting residents of the next canyon. When the river's route turned, the water wall bounced back upon itself, creating an ebb and flow similar to enormous waves in the nearby Pacific Ocean.

The devastation was nearly complete; few survived that initial surge, although those who did live watched their children or parents or friends swallowed up by the oncoming tide, listened to the roar as they held on to a pole, and smelled the mud as they clung to a limb on a high, sturdy tree. Great flashes not unlike lightning broke the dark of the night when the huge towers carrying electricity south toppled as if mere sticks and the 110-kilovolt lines they held snapped. The powerhouses were overwhelmed by the moving tide, swamped by the waves of water.

The first indication in Los Angeles of a problem occurred a few minutes later when half of the city went dark, relighted, and then went dark again. On the Southern California Edison monitoring boards, the high-voltage lines from the dam area went to zero.

The reaction was to try to telephone fieldworkers in the area of the dam to determine what had happened. And then, when they finally figured it out, to send for their superiors, all the way up to William Mulholland, to figure out what to do next.

Warnings went out haphazardly throughout Ventura County—a call made to one electrical station might not be passed on to the next. And calls made to police and sheriff's stations along the route of the Santa Clara River sometimes went unanswered in the early morning hours. Even so, the real problem was that few believed that the dam had collapsed or that the water would reach as far as their homes.

As word spread, some headed to the hills with what they could carry. Others stood on bridges waiting to watch the arrival of the flood, not realizing that they were about to be swept up in its tide, as was everything else in its path.

According to the investigative accounts later, there were many heroic acts during this time. In Santa Paula a highway patrolman got on his motorcycle and roamed the streets warning people of the impending flood, waking residents in the middle of the night, demanding they pay attention to the danger. Others organized caravans of cars to higher ground or went out toward the oncoming tide to save unsuspecting residents in the more rural canyons to the east.

And there were tales of people caught in the embarrassing position of having been wakened as the flood swept them up, naked, and deposited them in a tree, to be found later by rescuers; modesty gave way to survival in those terribly frightening moments.

The water kept coming, albeit at an increasingly slower rate of speed, but still high enough to do significant damage. In Santa Paula, after repeated warnings to leave, those standing on the bridges above the river realized at the last minute that they had better move off that overpass. Within moments the bridge was gone, taken down by the force of the flood. Houses were torn off their foundations, while others nearby were never touched. The flood followed the rules of nature, and those lucky enough to be on slightly higher ground were left unharmed.

The Santa Clara River Valley was in ruins, both its natural habitat and human construction devastated by the sudden movement of a large lake let loose by the faulty design of the dam. Grief and despair, and a healthy dose of anti-Los Angeles sentiment filled the hearts and minds of the people of Ventura County. Their original fears of water theft ironically turned out to be without merit. But their imaginations never included a bursting dam, and in the hours and days that followed the flood, as the residents turned to their leaders for aid and guidance, the horror of that night took its emotional toll.

The government of Los Angeles, remarkably, took immediate responsibility—remarkable because of its history of irresponsible actions in Owens Valley. The city council placed $1 million at the disposal of the Los Angeles Water and Power to settle claims, and it sent additional aid in the form of workers, materials, and equipment.

The area was ripe for the legal pickings. Unscrupulous attorneys throughout the state showed up to sign people to representation contracts of questionable merit. To keep a near-chaotic situation from getting worse, a Ventura County committee of local business and governmental leaders was established to create order; they were empowered to settle claims, rather than using the court system to adjudicate. In fact the committee coerced out-of-county attorneys to drop lawsuits filed on behalf of local residents.

Meanwhile, a variety of investigations were held into why the dam broke. LAWP, through Mulholland and his underlings, maintained that there had been no hint of a problem brewing, and that they had done all that they could to protect the citizenry downstream from the dam. But there were unanswered questions about the design of the dam, the quality of its construction, and the actual cause of the burst. Many pointed to the weakness of the western abutment, but nothing could be definitively proven. Then, in a remarkable book on the disaster, *Man-Made Disaster: The Story of the St. Francis Dam,* Charles Outland brought the research together and concluded that the western abutment was not the weak link in the dam's structure, but that it was the eastern wall instead.

In the end, with the water wars of the Owens Valley over, the dam was no longer needed as a storage area for Los Angeles. And although Los Angeles continued to grow and to thirst for more and more water, replacement of the dam was never seriously considered, and Southern California looked instead to other areas of the state to meet its insatiable needs. Today, the Owens Valley is still a dry wasteland, the Santa Clara Valley barely remembers the devastation of the flood of 1928, and Los Angeles thrives on water sent via aqueducts from the Colorado River and northern California watershed. While bombs and guns are no longer the method of warfare, the water wars continue and will continue as long as there are ways for growth in the Southern California desert.

CHAPTER 8

Friendly Fire

PORT CHICAGO EXPLOSION
- 1944 -

WHEN THE JAPANESE AIR FORCE ATTACKED PEARL Harbor, the U.S. Navy was dealt a severe blow to its strength. A great effort was made to replace and expand the naval fleet to fight on both the Atlantic and Pacific fronts. The Navy played key roles in ocean warfare and in safely delivering men and matériel on time to the battlefronts in Africa, Europe, and Asia.

To make these operations possible, the Navy developed several types of watercraft that could meet the needs of battle and supply.

This view of the ammunition explosion damage looks north, showing the wreckage of Building A-7 (Joiner Shop) in the center and ship pier beyond. Note the bulldozer and damaged automobiles in the foreground, railway crane at left, and scattered pilings. Photo taken by Mare Island Navy Yard, courtesy Naval Historical Center

How Ammunition Got to the Battlefield from Port Arthur

1. The War Department notified the Bureau of Ordnance, an agency of the U.S. Navy.
2. The Bureau of Ordnance sent a detailed list of what ammunition needed to be where at what time to the Service Force Subordinate Command.
3. The SFSC requested the port director to have the ships needed prepared for loading by inspecting them to make sure they were ocean ready.
4. The port director, in coordination with the SFSC and the base commander, developed a loading schedule and applied for the necessary permits from the captain of the port.
5. The captain of the port inspected each ship for possible hazards and for their ability to safely load ammunition. He, or his representative, had the ability to stop loading at any time if he saw and was unable to correct practices considered unsafe.
6. The magazine planning officer developed a loading work sheet for each ship.
7. The magazine transportation officer coordinated the arrival of railcars with the ammunition at the 18-foot loading platform.
8. Ordnance battalions made up of one hundred men, were divided into five twenty-man platoons, one for each hatch in the ship who would handle the munitions once they were hoisted or conveyed into the holds.
9. Ten of the men in each platoon moved material from the boxcar to the net for hoisting; the other ten men moved the cargo out of the net and to its storage space.
10. There were winch operators, signalmen, checkers, hatch tenders, and carpenters mates, as well as junior and senior officers.

11. The men were required to move a minimum of ten tons per hour, and worked three days on, one day in the barracks, three days on, and overnight liberty. They received a lunch break on each shift.
12. Ammunition was loaded twenty-four hours per day, seven days a week.

Source: Regina T. Akers, "The Port Chicago Mutiny, 1944," in Naval Mutinies of the Twentieth Century: An International Perspective, *Christopher M. Bell and Bruce A. Ellman, eds., p. 198 (London: Frank Cass,* 2003)

Among these were the "Liberty Ships," speedily built and easy-to-load supply ships that came to play a crucial role in bringing needed equipment and armaments to warships to keep those crafts ready for battle.

Existing ammunition depots were unable to handle the number of ships that were constantly being loaded and sent out to sea. So the Navy established a large depot near the town of Port Chicago on the Sacramento River at Suisun Bay, about 35 miles east of San Francisco. This enormous depot was capable of handling deliveries from three railroads and, after May 1944, the loading of two ships (instead of one) simultaneously in three shifts, covering all twenty-four hours of the day and night.

The armed forces of the United States maintained a policy of race segregation. Following both written and unwritten rules, each military branch kept nonwhites out of both leadership roles and fighting units. There were rules on how many African Americans could be in each service branch: 10 percent was the maximum. And there were rules about what assignments were available to African Americans.

The Navy limited African Americans to cook, steward, and other mess positions at the beginning of the war. President Franklin Roosevelt pressured the General Board of the Navy to allow them to be in stevedore and construction and other working noncombatant battalions. Few were allowed on ships. And even fewer were commissioned during the four years of the war.

Already resentful about being left out of the fighting, the workers at Port Chicago had to endure oppressive conditions. Paid less and worked hard, they loaded ships with armaments without first being trained on how to handle explosives. Similar jobs in civilian life required significant training; for instance, two years of experience was required for winch drivers before they could work on their own. And while the U.S. Coast Guard developed a manual for handling dangerous cargo, the Navy never designed a way for the men to do likewise.

The Navy also refused an offer from union officials to train the men. The officers believed that only on-the-job training was necessary for people who they described as "uneducated," "unreliable," "emotional," and lacking the "capacity to understand or remember orders or instructions."

Commander of the Port Chicago facility, Capt. Merrill T. Kinne, not only insisted on a minimum loading of ten tons per hour, he posted the tonnage loads for each platoon on a chalkboard to foster competition for swiftness without regard to safety. Junior officers bet on the speed of platoons and egged them on.

Workers complained constantly that bombs were being bounced onto the deck or against other bombs and ammunition. But they were assured that without detonators, the munitions were harmless. And until the night of July 17, 1944, that had been shown to be correct.

That night, two ships were being loaded at the pier, the SS *E. A. Bryan* and the SS *Quinalt Victory*. The *Bryan* had been in port for a few days and had been loaded with 4,485 tons of ammunition and high explosives. Thirteen boxcars were waiting to be loaded onto the two ships. The Navy was shipping in this load a new plastics-based torpedo, the Mark 47, to replace dynamite-based torpedoes.

At 10:19 P.M. two huge explosions, a few seconds apart, rocked the

Bay Area. Creating a blast equivalent to a magnitude 3.4 earthquake on the Richter scale, 5,000 tons of explosives combusted. Felt as far away as San Francisco, it created a fire that turned the sky red, and sent debris over 2 miles high.

Nothing was left of the pier, and the explosion destroyed the ships, boxcars filled with explosives and the locomotive attached to them, a barge, and the wharf, still under construction. The *E. A. Bryan* disappeared; the *Quinalt Victory* flew in the air for 500 feet and what was left—the stern—was found facing in the opposite direction from its loading dock. Every building on the base was damaged, as were the nearby towns of Port Chicago, Concord, and Pittsburg.

The loss in human life was as tremendous as it was tragic. The death toll reached 320, of whom 202 were enlisted men loading the ships. That meant that nearly two-thirds of the dead were African Americans, or roughly one-sixth of the total casualties of African Americans in the U.S. Navy during World War II. Another 390 on the base were injured, of whom 226 were African American. But most of all, those who were nearby and came to help suffered from shock and depression from the sight and from cleaning up. They searched the rubble for three days, but only fifty-one bodies could be identified.

Kinne commended the 200 African-American men who had helped in cleaning up the site, including four who put out a fire in nearby boxcars that had not exploded. But most if not all of the men were traumatized.

A court of inquiry, established on July 20, interviewed 125 witnesses over six weeks in an attempt to establish the cause of the accident. However, only five African-American servicemen were called to testify. In its report the court exonerated the officers, all of whom were white, and implied that the servicemen handling the ammunition had to have done something wrong. The court did note that the loading of ammunition should never be "a matter for competition," an obvious slap on the wrist to Captain Kinne's blackboard totals.

This view looks south from the ship pier, showing the wreckage of Building A-7 (Joiner Shop) at the right. There is a piece of twisted steel plating just to the left of the long pole in left center.
Photo taken by Mare Island Navy Yard, courtesy Naval Historical Center

The unidentifiable remains were buried in a local cemetery with tombstones that read UNKNOWN US NAVY 17 JULY 1944. While the Navy recommended a $5,000 bereavement payment to each family, Mississippi Congressman John Rankin objected because most of the dead were black. After a compromise, Congress awarded $3,000.

The other men had been transferred to Camp Shoemaker in Oakland. While white military personnel from Port Chicago were granted leave, African Americans were not. On barracks duty only, they were not asked at first to load ships. Scared and nervous, the slightest noise could make them jump. Many hoped and believed that they would be permanently transferred from that duty. But then two divisions were sent to Mare Island Ammunition Depot in nearby Vallejo.

On August 9 the men were ordered to load ammunition again.

Fearing for their lives and wanting proper training, 328 men initially refused, willing to risk the punishment of a court-martial rather than to chance dying in another explosion. But after warnings and threats, seventy of their number returned to work. After being arrested and held on a barge for three days, the remaining men were warned again that they faced serious charges for their refusal to follow orders. They were threatened with charges of mutiny, but more immediately they were threatened by guards who said they would shoot them on the spot. In the end fifty held their position; the others returned to work. The men who returned to work received courts-martial, bad conduct discharges, and loss of three months' pay.

The fifty holdouts were taken back to Camp Shoemaker for questioning. At no time were they offered an attorney or told that they did not have to sign anything. No one read them the official definition of mutiny so that they could determine if they were being mutinous. The questions they were asked were designed to prove mutiny, not to determine if they had violated the law. Officers made some of the men sign blank statement sheets, which were filled in after the fact by the officers themselves.

For their act of refusal to load the ships, the Navy had the option of charging them with failure to follow orders, a much less serious charge. But the prosecution argued that the men had conspired not just to stop work but to mutiny. Each man testified, explaining why he had refused to return to his job. A psychologist testified to the traumatic condition of the men. And the defense argued that the men never actually received a direct order to return to work.

The seven whites that made up the jury took eighty minutes to find the fifty men guilty of conspiracy to commit mutiny. They were sentenced to prison for terms ranging from eight to fifteen years.

Support for the fifty seamen began with the trial. Thurgood Marshall, who at the time was the head of the NAACP Legal Defense Fund, led that organization's campaign to overturn the verdict. Black churches and media were vocal supporters. Eleanor Roosevelt pressured Secretary of the Navy Forrestal, who, finally, in 1946, released all of the men, assigning them to ships serving in the South Pacific. Eventually, all were dishonorably discharged, making them ineligible for veteran's benefits and leaving a mark on their records.

But certain changes did occur, and some of them may have been directly caused by the stand of these men. Certainly, this case brought to the fore the segregationist practices of the Navy. To counter the belief that it had been biased, the Navy assigned whites to load ammunition ships along with the original contingent of African Americans, forcing the navy to provide proper training for all involved. And the case may have accelerated the desegregation of the military by making public the discrimination.

The men stood first and foremost not as African Americans but as seamen. And if nothing else, the Navy took a hard look at its loading practices and made dramatic changes. It even reformulated the Mark 47, which is believed to have been too unstable for the type of handling necessary to get it onto the ships, let alone into the holds of the submarines that would actually fire these torpedoes. It is believed that this saved countless lives of Americans on ships around the world.

President Harry Truman issued an executive order desegregating the armed forces in 1948. African Americans have been given opportunities since then to participate fully in the military. Tensions continue to exist throughout the military around race, but they are more a reflection of the country as a whole.

In 1980 Port Chicago was incorporated into the Concord Naval Weapons Station. A plaque to commemorate the loss of life at Port Chicago on July 17, 1944, lists the names of all who died in the explosion. Their lives, and those of the men court-martialed and imprisoned, were among those sacrificed in the fight to end racial discrimination in the United States.

CHAPTER 9

Trapped by Flame

RATTLESNAKE FOREST FIRE
- 1953 -

GRINDSTONE CANYON, NEAR RATTLESNAKE RIDGE, sits several miles northwest of Elk Creek, a small town on State Route 162 on the Sacramento Valley side of the Mendocino National Forest. The hills in this area, many covered by decades-old chaparral, rise to about 2,400 feet, some at quite a steep angle. On July 9, 1953, at about 2:40 P.M., a brush fire was reported out of control in the canyon.

Behind this memorial to firefighters who died in the Rattlesnake Fire, note the crosses on the hills in background where their bodies were found.
Larry Cregger, U.S. Forest Service

This was the second fire reported in the general area that day. The first, now known as the Hull or Chrome Fire, was on nearby state-protected lands. Investigators had determined that the fire, quickly contained in an eleven-acre area, had been set using an incendiary device.

On his way back from fighting that fire, A. B. Miller, a member of Fire Prevention Aid, noticed a fire approximately 25 feet by 30 feet in size at Oleta Point near Powder House Creek. After notifying the Elk Creek Butte fire station, he returned to the fire to try to contain it. He was joined there by a suppression crew, which immediately began to cut a fire line to contain the blaze along its south flank.

Another crew of eight men joined the work. Additionally, Forest Service Assistant C. C. Lafferty and engineer J. M. Ewing also arrived. All too soon, the area became too hot to continue the line construction, and Ewing pulled the crews off the south flank and sent them to the head of the fire. He had seen that the fire had moved west about a mile up the ridge in the direction of Rattlesnake Ridge. He devised a plan of direct attack to head off further movement in that direction while burning out the brush to a nearby road, thus making the road and existing firebreak lines the containment perimeter on the northern, eastern, and southern borders.

The head of the fire had moved onto Rattlesnake Ridge, but the crews were successful in controlling it. The main fire was considered contained early in the evening. However, spot fires (fires that start away from the main fires) flared in various areas along the other borders, and all were contained—at first.

A testy spot fire began about 8:15 P.M. about 300 feet from Powder House Ridge along the slope down to Powder House Creek. Twenty-four men worked for two hours to contain the fire. They had finished a line around the spot and took a lunch break in an area out of sight of the main fire. Two of the crew leaders went up to the site of the spot fire to view the main fire, and when they returned to the eating area, discussions were held on alternatives now that they had finished their assignment.

Without a lookout and without assessing their own position for safety, the men found themselves in a bind when, suddenly, at about 10:15 P.M., the winds changed direction, and the spot fire exploded up the slope. It moved uphill northeast, then downhill southeast rapidly. Fires ordinarily move uphill; cooler evening temperatures will direct a fire downhill at a very slow rate of speed. Eyewitnesses stood in disbelief as the fire sped quickly toward the canyon floor.

Lafferty, seeing that the path of the fire was toward the men, ran down to alert the two-dozen workers. He yelled to them, but the men below may not have heard or understood him. Nine men headed uphill toward the firefighter, and they were saved. Fifteen others made their way eastward down the slope of the hill into the canyon, trying to outrun the fire. But the brush was thicker and more difficult to traverse, and within fifteen minutes the rapidly moving flames had caught up with the escaping men.

For the next few hours, other firefighters searched areas away from the fire's path in the hopes that some or all of the men had escaped. But the fire area itself was too hot to enter until early morning. Finally, the searchers entered the fire zone, finding the first burned body around the first light of dawn. By 8:30 A.M., all missing persons were accounted for: fifteen dead.

The fire continued to grow and consume. It took another day and a half to finally contain the fire and force it to burn itself out. Thirteen hundred acres were scorched.

Stanford Philip Pattan, son of a locally well-known forest firefighter, Phil Pattan, was down on his luck. Behind in the rent and car payments, out of work, with a pregnant wife and three kids to support, Pattan was troubled. But when his wife figured out how much debt was involved, she walked out on him, taking the children, telling

Stanford that he had to clear things up before she came back.

Pattan looked for work throughout the Willows area of the Sacramento Valley, but no one would hire him. And though he had been turned down for a job at the lumber mill near the national forest, he decided on July 9 to make another visit there to ask again. The only thing was, he never got there.

He had been trained as a forest firefighter just like his dad, but he could not get hired on as a regular; he was called on occasionally as temporary crew. He told fire investigators later that he needed a job, so he decided to start a fire. Not an uncommon occurrence, these "job fires" have been known to be devastating.

Pattan drove up into the hills in late morning as if he were going to the lumber mill. Instead, he sat alongside the road and looked at the thick underbrush that had grown up in the canyon, he later told John Maclean for his book *Fire and Ashes*. He remembered others criticizing the National Forest Service policy of stopping all fires because it allowed all this untended growth of chaparral that made hiking, hunting, and fishing nearly impossible in many canyons in these hills. He took out a box of matches, lit one, and threw it into the brush. Then he drove over to a nearby resident's house to watch it burn.

He made himself very visible all afternoon, showing up at the Elk Creek Butte lookout and at a local bar. But he was miffed when the fire was contained within a couple of hours. So he set out again, and at Oleta Point he repeated what he had done on Hull Road at Chrome. And another fire started. This time, the fire caught quickly and moved up the ridge slope at a good pace.

With the fire going and the alarm sounded, he went to get a job. But the Forest Service told him that the fire was small enough that they weren't hiring. Later, they hired Pattan as a cook for the night. Although angry at this snub of his skills, he took the job nonetheless. And it was here that investigators came to find him.

Under today's rules of interrogation, Pattan would have been afforded more protection from the onslaught of questioning that he endured. He eventually confessed, explaining his situation and how he didn't expect anyone to get hurt. He just wanted a job.

Although the charges against Pattan were originally second-degree murder, they were reduced by the grand jury, which could not find premeditation—a necessary ingredient in the legal definition of murder—to two counts of willful burning. He pled guilty and was sentenced to two consecutive terms of one to ten years. He served three years, and then he was paroled back to his hometown of Willows.

The New Tribes Mission was about 25 miles south of the fire in the Mendocino National Forest. The mission, an evangelical Christian missionary school, as part of its teaching of community service offered authorities prospective missionaries to help fight forest fires. And as is usual in this area, when the fires broke out, the mission was called. It sent a group of volunteers.

Fourteen of the fifteen dead firefighters were New Tribes missionaries.

How was it that well-trained staff and volunteers lost their lives in just a few quick moments in what was otherwise a routine fire event? The answers were complex: Weather, terrain, and procedural problems all combined to cause this disaster.

The terrain of the national forest was hilly. Between the ridges and buttes, which were covered with chaparral lightly mixed with a variety of grasses, were canyons with thicker and denser growth of chamise, grass, oaks, pines, and other flora. In fact the northeast sides of the canyons had less growth than the southeast sides.

As is typical of California in July, the weather was warm and sunny; no rain had fallen in weeks. The important variable in the mountains was the direction and strength of wind currents at various times of the day, because the wind provided oxygen to the fire and directed its movement.

During the day thermal heating of the canyon floors created an updraft, and the fire followed the direction of the wind, burning up the slopes of Powder House and Rattlesnake Ridges. But as the sun set in the mountains, starting around 9:00 P.M., the heating process ended, and the winds calmed. Firefighters and other witnesses noticed that the fire stagnated as the winds died down.

Then, as the canyon floor cooled, the warmer air rose and the cooler denser air dropped toward the canyon. The wind shifted to a down-slope direction, and the fire burned again, but this time it headed down into the canyons. And because the western mountains were warmer, the cooler air directed the fire to move slowly in an eastward direction.

Yet the fire burst as if it had exploded. And then it ran rapidly downhill. The variable that had not been considered was that a changing weather front had formed over the coast, and at the very time that the mountains began to cool, the system moved over the ridge. This change in pressure was responsible for the sudden and rapid movement downhill.

So the men, who were grouped toward the canyon floor on the western side of the ridge, found themselves caught by the forces created by wind, weather, and topography that were not taken into account in their training. Additionally, it has been speculated that those fighting the main fire and other spot fires forgot about the men from New Tribe Mission as they focused on their own crises. And lastly, the firefighters themselves had made a decision, based on being tired and hungry, to stay in the canyon and eat their lunch instead of walking a relatively few paces to a safer area.

From this tragedy, a new understanding of mountain-area forest fires grew. With that knowledge changes were made in training and procedures that have successfully protected wildfire fighters throughout the United States. Today, the Mendocino Rattlesnake Fire is used as a case study in training staff of the California Department of Forestry and other firefighting organizations around the country.

CHAPTER 10

Rains That Wouldn't Stop

SANTA CRUZ CHRISTMAS FLOOD
- 1955 -

MOST OF CALIFORNIA HAS TWO SEASONS: DRY AND wet. The dry season runs from about April to October, and the wet season is from November to March. Sometimes, the rains never seem to arrive, bringing drought conditions to the area. But occasionally the weather patterns are such that the clouds seem to drop everything they hold. December of 1955 falls into the latter category.

The troubles began on December 13. Over a two-day period, a strong high-pressure system developed over Alaska, moving into

Federal, state, and local officials are shown examining the flood-damaged Soquel Bridge. Santa Cruz Public Libraries

Canada, while a strong low-pressure storm system brewed off the Oregon coast. As these systems slowly moved eastward, light rain was reported along the northern California coast. While these systems formed, an upper-level flow of warm moist air from the Hawaiian Islands area of the Pacific Ocean strengthened, and as it gained strength it brought more and more precipitation to northern coastal areas.

Within a few days high-pressure systems surrounded the storm system, keeping it stationary. The upper-level winds, sometimes as strong as 115 miles per hour, pushed the tropical air into California, and the deluge began. For five days, starting on December 19, the rains, torrential and unrelenting, attacked the central and northern regions of California.

With the rains came the winds. In the Sierra Nevada range, winds were clocked as high as 90 miles per hour. The San Francisco Bay suffered 75 mile-per-hour gusts. The barometric pressure fell to 29.00 and in some areas below that. The northern half of the state was under siege.

This storm came in after several light storms in November and early December. The ground had already absorbed the precipitation from those rains. In the Sierras the snowpack was about 6 feet, normal for that time of year. Because this new storm was so warm—freezing altitude moved from 5,000 feet to 7,000 feet and finally to 10,000 feet—the water content of the snow was increased, but for the first five days, there was no significant increase in the snow pack.

During the ten days from December 17 to December 26—the worst of the precipitation—the rains demonstrated a pattern of a few hours of excessive rain followed by light rain for short periods. The storms then tapered off until they finally ended December 28.

For the first two days, the rains were light in the inland valleys of northern and central California. Then a large storm came through, dropping as much as six inches in some areas. Another lull ensued with light precipitation. But for two and a half days, beginning on

December 21, the intensity increased, averaging over seven inches in some mountain areas.

Along the coast the pattern was similar. Less than two inches fell in Marin and Mendocino counties, and less than one in San Mateo and Santa Cruz counties. But starting on December 19, the rains intensified, dropping six and a half inches in Oakville, in Napa County, and over nine inches in parts of Santa Cruz County.

December 20 and 21 brought a relative lull, with only an inch or two falling, less on the southern end and more on the northern end of these regions. The respite, however, was short-lived.

December 22 changed everything, with the storms pounding the coast, especially around Marin and Mendocino counties, where seven and nine inches fell, respectively. Santa Cruz and as far south as Big Sur saw dramatic increases as well. The upper San Lorenzo Valley area of Santa Cruz received four inches on December 22 and a whopping eleven inches on December 23.

The storm system was now moving in a southeasterly direction, hitting Monterey County and into San Luis Obispo County. Big Sur registered seven inches on December 23. Santa Margarita, in San Luis Obispo County, received almost five and a half inches on December 24.

The rains began to subside after Christmas Eve, but it continued to rain until December 28. By that time the damage had been done. The saturated ground refused the excess water, sending the surplus into the streams, rivers, and lakes throughout central and northern California. The rivers filled to capacity and overflowed. Flooding started in the mountains and grew to devastating proportions as it moved toward cities in the Sacramento Valley and along the coast.

The hardest hit in the Sacramento Valley area were the twin cities of Marysville and Yuba City, 40 miles north of the state capital. The cities face each other over the Feather River, near the confluence of the Feather and Yuba Rivers. On December 24, the Feather River broke through its levee at the Shanghai Bend, south of Yuba City.

The city was 95 percent underwater to maximum depths of as much as 12 feet. Three thousand homes were flooded. On the eastern side of the river, Marysville was also endangered—to within inches of its protective levees—by the Yuba, which had overflowed its banks at the New Bullards Bar and Englebright Reservoir Dams. Thirty thousand people from the two cities had to be evacuated, and thirty-eight people died. In total the Sacramento Valley area saw 360,000 acres underwater.

While many rivers and creeks overflowed their banks and levees—from the Klamath in the north to Alameda Creek in the East Bay Area—the other major population area to take a beating was Santa Cruz County. With as much as eighteen inches of rain in the first five days of the storm, the water ran off into the streams leading to the San Lorenzo River, which starts high in the Santa Cruz Mountains and meanders down to Monterey Bay. The river stopped up, clogged with debris as torrents of water rushed down its narrow channel, destroying nearly a hundred mountain homes along the way.

Finally, at about 10:00 P.M. on December 22, the river came over its banks as it passed by the city of Santa Cruz. Downtown sits in a basin, and the waters rose several feet deep throughout the plain. Nearly every downtown business suffered water damage; the county government, which had many of its documents stored in the basement of the Cooper House on the corner of Pacific and Church Streets, suffered great losses. To the east of the river, the neighborhood between the river and Branciforte Creek had also flooded, taking many homes off their foundations. Two thousand Santa Cruz residents were evacuated.

Also in Santa Cruz County, the town of Soquel, near the outlet of Soquel Creek, faced a logjam of debris as four cabins and a house were swept down the creek by the waters, piling up against the Soquel Bridge. The creek backed up, and water was diverted into the town itself, flooding businesses and homes. The Watsonville area, which sits beside the Pajaro River, also was flooded. Ironically, new levees had just been built to protect Watsonville from this type of situation.

The rains abated for a while but came again in January. After another three weeks of intermittent storms, none as bad as those of the December deluge, the rains tapered off. In the end two-thirds of the state had been affected, sixty-seven people had died, and damages hit $166 million.

In the aftermath of the floods, new levees were built and new water management plans were drafted and implemented. But the floods have returned to the Sacramento Valley again and again, especially in the area of Yuba City. In 1964, 1986, and 1997, the Feather and Yuba Rivers flooded or threatened to flood. Yet the cities continue to build out into the floodplain, even with the threat of more floods.

Santa Cruz, following a plan devised by the Army Corps of Engineers, rebuilt the banks of the San Lorenzo River through the downtown area. But the plan was faulty, and in 1982 the city was again endangered when the river rose so high that it threatened to come over its banks. It did destroy one overpass, taking out the electricity and emergency communication systems serving an extensive area. The major problem with the design seemed to be that the new, lower level of the riverbed silted up. New work has been completed that hopefully will protect the river and the city.

Soquel residents, at first interested in a corps' plan to protect the town, later rejected it because an earth-filled dam was a key component of the corps' strategy. Although a dam would have prevented the amount of water that reached the town from heading downstream, the residents felt a dam would destroy wildlife and would be unsafe in an earthquake-prone area.

Californians tend to place themselves in the path of changeable weather patterns and their effects, and the economics and politics of water cannot be overestimated within the state. Harnessing nature's resources continues to be key to California's growth, from the inland Salton Sea to the agricultural riches of the Sacramento Valley. At the same time, it is the belief that nature can be harnessed that often places California residents at risk.

CHAPTER 11
Wall of Water
CRESCENT CITY TSUNAMI
- 1964 -

CRESCENT CITY, CALIFORNIA, IN 1964 WAS A SMALL logging and fishing town about 30 miles south of the Oregon border. Originally established as a port, it served as a supply depot for gold prospectors during the Gold Rush. After the tide of prospectors petered out, the residents turned to fishing and lumber, the two natural resources of this area, to sustain the town's economy.

Many houses not bolted to their foundations were swept away and destroyed by the force of the tsunami's impact. Del Norte County Historical Society Photograph

Tsunami sightings had been recorded along this part of the coast since 1855. Most of them had resulted little damage, and only a handful had been caused by local earthquakes. Teletsunamis (those caused by distant earthquakes) were more common, and residents had become rather complacent after many alerts and warnings that had proved to be of no consequence.

Just before midnight on March 27, 1964, however, Crescent City citizens learned what it means to be hit by a tsunami. An earthquake more than 2,000 miles away washed away their complacency forever.

The earthquake, the second largest at the time, occurred at 5:36 P.M., Alaska standard time (6:36 Pacific standard time) more than 10 miles under the ocean about 75 miles east of Anchorage, Alaska, and 55 miles west of Valdez in the Prince William Sound area. Registering magnitude 9.2 on the Richter scale at its peak, its rupture was 500 miles long and 150 miles wide. The land rose over 30 feet in some areas and dropped as much as 7 feet in others. The Pacific tectonic plate moved about 25 feet north under the American plate.

The quake lasted more than four minutes, devastating downtown Anchorage (Fourth Avenue sank more than 10 feet) and destroying gas and water lines. The cost of the damage was over $300 million. Outside of Anchorage, where population is sparse, landslides blocked rail and auto roads. In Seward, Alaska, the rail yard and seaport were destroyed.

Yet the worst damage was yet to come. The quake's up-and-down rupture caused several regional and local tsunamis. Locally, a tsunami wave that went through the Straits of Valdez reached a height of over 200 feet, and it killed more than one hundred people.

The waves continued down the coast of North America, striking hard in British Columbia, Washington, and Oregon, where they killed four at Newport. The first wave reached the California-Oregon border and Crescent City at 11:52 P.M., PST.

Don't Call a Tsunami a Tidal Wave!

What is the difference between a tidal wave and a tsunami? A *tidal wave* is caused by the relationship of the moon and earth (lunar tides) and specific weather conditions. Storm conditions cause the waters to swell, and added to a high tide the levels of the ocean rise.

A *tsunami* is caused by the movement of one tectonic plate under or over another plate under the ocean. The rise or drop of the underwater land pushes the water up and out away from the fault. One or more waves result from this earth movement. In deep-ocean the pulse wave travels at great speed—as much as 550 miles per hour. As the topography changes on the approach to shore, the shallower area causes the wave to slow down. But that same shallowness forces the water up over the ambient sea level (which is controlled by the lunar tides). By the time the wave reaches shore, it can loom as high as 2,000 feet above the surface of the ocean.

Civil Defense officials received a telex warning them of a "probable" wave that was "unconfirmed." The time was just after 11:00 P.M. With insufficient information and little lead time, officials could not decide what to do. Acting on false alarms in the past had brought recriminations from locals.

The first wave came with high tide, pushing the water up an additional 8 feet from the 6 feet that had been expected that evening. While far from devastating, it alarmed many residents, who evacuated to higher ground. But it had been a minor rise and had done little more than deposit debris on the beach at the foot of Front Street. By the time the second wave came, about a half-hour later, the harbor had been emptied. But this wave was even smaller than the first, cresting at about 4 feet, and didn't get as far up the beach.

Thinking the worst was over, some residents decided to return home or to see the damage for themselves. No one realized the peril until it was too late. An hour after the second wave, a third and much larger wave hit town. Reaching 16 feet above ambient tide (22 feet in all), the wave crashed over the seawall and into town. Then a fourth wave, smaller yet still destructive, struck.

Seven people were partying at the Long Branch Tavern when the first wave hit. They left, but because the second wave was smaller, the group decided to return to the bar to continue the celebration. The third wave hit them hard, pushing them back 300 feet into Elk Creek. Climbing out onto the roof, two of the men decided to get their boat, which was nearby. All seven got into the boat and rowed toward higher ground. But just a few boat lengths from shore, the fourth wave hit. Only two people survived by grabbing hold of the Highway 101 bridge as the boat passed under it.

One couple, the Londons, received a late-night visit from friends who came to warn them of the tsunami's approach. Deciding that they were no longer in imminent danger, the friends stayed for coffee, which was served at 1:00 A.M. They never finished their cup of java. The third wave slammed into the Londons' house; one person died and another was severely injured.

The local shoemaker's shop and residence was swamped; the shoemaker drowned. A woman with two children attempted to escape, but the water swept both children away to their deaths.

Water is not the only destructive force in a tsunami. The waves carry the debris of ocean and land over which they have traveled. Trees that are swept away en route compound the water's wrath, giving it power to strike not only with its own dense, black liquidity but also with battering rams that crush autos and damage buildings.

One wave picked up a gasoline truck at the local Huskey-Texaco distribution depot and pushed it into electrical wires. The subsequent fire took three days to put out. The Union Oil storage plant also caught fire.

Communications among emergency and police officials along the coast from Alaska to Los Angeles were poor. One civil defense worker said that they had received a telex warning them of a tsunami, but no one seemed to know what to expect. And while most tsunamis hit only once, this one came in four distinct waves. After the fourth wave came and went, no one knew whether more were on their way.

During the night looting began, and the small police force, with the aid of volunteers, worked to prevent further loss and to detain looters. In the morning Governor Edmund "Pat" Brown sent in the National Guard.

As dawn approached, people in and around Crescent City were able to see the devastation. The waterfront area was demolished, as was the part of downtown closest to the ocean. In all, twenty-nine businesses were totally destroyed. Houses not bolted to their foundations were moved away by the water. For miles along Highway 101, fallen trees and branches and landslides littered the road, making access to Crescent City difficult.

Crescent City was not the only California harbor to feel the water's force. Marin County and San Francisco marinas saw boats and floating piers break loose, causing extensive damage. In Santa Cruz harbor, a hydraulic dredge sank and floating piers were damaged. Other coastal ports as far away as Los Angeles and Long Beach suffered as well.

Within a few days, the Huskey-Texaco and Union Oil plant fires were extinguished, roads and streets were cleaned and reopened, and leaking butane tanks were sealed. In the end about 150 businesses were destroyed or damaged, and the Coast Guard Station was taken by the waves. The damage totaled $7.4 million with eleven dead in this area. The rest of the state saw about $2 million in additional damage.

The painful process of reconstruction is well documented in *The Raging Sea,* by Dennis M. Powers, whose detailed descriptions from survivors bring home the power of this tsunami's devastation. While much of Crescent City was rebuilt, the psyche of the town was forever damaged. Signs direct visitors and locals alike to evacuation routes. The lumber and fishing industries were damaged almost beyond repair (changing economic conditions that have taken place over the last four decades subsequently contributed to their demise).

Crescent City received the worst damage because of the way it is situated geographically. Geologists say that the underwater topography of the ocean focuses the waves directly on Crescent City, making it a "magnet" for tsunamis. Had the town been laid out facing in a different way, it would have been missed by the wave completely.

Geologists also have discovered that this was not the worst tsunami to hit Crescent City. In 1700 an earthquake estimated above magnitude 9 was so great that coastal forests were completely submerged and tsunamis destroyed houses as far away as Japan.

In 1996 Congress established the National Tsunami Hazard Mitigation Program. Six sensors have been placed along the Pacific coast in deep-ocean from Alaska to South America to immediately warn of the potential for tsunami from large quakes. Since a tsunami can travel at over 500 miles per hour, warnings must be quickly disseminated to give local authorities optimum time to evacuate low-lying areas.

The problem, however, is that only certain types of earthquakes cause tsunamis. Scientists must quickly assess their other data to determine if a tsunami is likely to develop. If not, the warning is canceled. This is what happened in 2005 when a magnitude 7.2 quake occurred off the coast of Crescent City itself. The warning signal was triggered by the size of the quake, and a warning was issued publicly. But an hour later it was determined that a thrust fault had not occurred, and the warning was canceled.

Is California safer now from tsunamis than it was in 1964? Decidedly yes—and no. The present warning system definitely gives coastline residents a chance to escape, depending on where the earthquake occurs. And construction codes have been changed to provide greater earthquake safety, which includes the anchoring of houses and buildings to their foundations; lack of anchoring contributed significantly to the loss in 1964.

But an important part of the hazard mitigation program relies on the proper mapping of coastline and developing of evacuation plans locally. Of the five states in or along the Pacific Ocean, California and Alaska lag in preparation, simply because of the amount of coastline that needs to be mapped.

The chances of more devastating tsunamis are great, especially in the Cascadia Subduction Zone, where both the Alaska (1964) and Crescent City (2005) earthquakes occurred. Residents who live along the coast and visitors to the area would be wise to stay alert for this sudden event—a matter of life and death.

CHAPTER 12
He Shot the Pilot
CRASHES OF PAL 773 AND PSA 1771
- 1964 and 1987 -

PACIFIC AIR LINES FLIGHT 773, RENO, NV, TO SAN FRANCISCO VIA STOCKTON, 1964. Francisco Gonzales had many problems, not the least of which was debt. A member of the 1960 Philippines Olympic yachting team, Gonzales lived in San Francisco with his wife and family. He often threatened their lives and the lives of others. At the

N350PS, the actual plane that crashed December 7, 1987. T. Quackenbush, Airliners.net beginning of May 1964, he told friends and relatives that he would die either on May 6 or May 7. On the evening of May 6, he bought a gun. On the morning of May 7, he used it.

He bought the gun and showed it to friends, telling them he was going to shoot himself. He bought two airline life insurance policies worth about $105,000—in those days available from a machine in the airport—and named his wife as beneficiary. Then he boarded a Pacific Air Lines (PAL) flight to Reno.

Gonzales spent the night in the gambling casinos of the "Biggest Little City in the World." At about 5:30 the next morning, he boarded PAL Flight 773 to San Francisco with a stop in Stockton, California. He was still carrying the gun, a Smith and Wesson .357 Magnum.

The plane, a Fairchild F-27 twin-turboprop, was the workhorse of many regional air fleets. It had a passenger section in the rear and a cargo hold between the passengers and the cockpit. Onboard that morning were thirty-three people and three crewmembers. The plane took off at 5:54 A.M. and landed in Stockton at 6:30 A.M. At the stop in Stockton, two passengers deplaned as ten came on. Only one of the forty-four people on the plane knew that it would never make it to San Francisco.

The plane returned to the air at 6:38 A.M., heading for San Francisco, ordinarily perhaps a twenty-minute flight. Ten minutes out, as the captain began his landing procedures, Gonzales gained entrance to the cargo area and shot the pilot and the copilot. "PAL 773, Skipper's shot . . . we've been shot . . . trying to help" came crackling over the headphones of the air traffic controllers in the SFO approach tower. The plane went down on a grassy hill near San Ramon in Contra Costa County. All forty-four people perished.

Investigators found the gun and the six used bullet casings. They also found that the plane was in "landing trim," and should have stayed at flying level for a time. But eyewitnesses said that the plane's nosedive was close to vertical, so Gonzales himself must have forced the plane down by exerting pressure on the yoke to be sure that the plane went down.

Gonzales was the first civilian to use a gun in the commission of a hijacking.

PACIFIC SOUTHWEST AIRLINES FLIGHT 1771 LOS ANGELES TO SAN FRANCISCO, 1987. David A. Burke, an employee of US Air, had been accused of stealing $68 from a drink fund that the flight attendants had established. Placed on unpaid leave during the investigation, Burke appeared at the US Air Board of Appeals on December 7, 1987, to plead for mercy. He took responsibility for the theft, asking for leniency since he was the sole support for his children. His supervisor, Raymond Thompson, dismissed him. According to investigative reports, as Burke left, Thompson's secretary told him to have a nice day. Burke allegedly replied, "I intend on having a very good day."

Raymond Thompson commuted to Los Angeles International Airport from his home in the San Francisco Bay Area every day, and December 7 was no different. He left his office and caught the 4:00 P.M. Pacific Southwest Airlines (PSA) Flight 1771, a British Aerospace Bae-146-200A jetliner. US Air had recently bought PSA, and all of the aircraft still had PSA smiles painted over the nose of the plane, thereby giving them the name "Smile of Stockton."

When Thompson sat down, he failed to notice the other passengers. Among them was David Burke, who had bought a ticket for the flight knowing that Thompson would be aboard. And unbeknownst to anyone else on the plane, Burke had boarded carrying a borrowed .44 Magnum revolver, having used his US Air identification badge, which he had failed to return to his former employer, to bypass the metal detectors at the gate.

Takeoff went smoothly, and soon the plane was cruising at 29,000 feet. Burke took out the airbag from the seat pocket and scrawled the following note: "Hi Ray. I think it's sort of ironical that we end up like this. I asked for some leniency for my family. Remember? Well, I got none and you'll get none."

As the plane cruised over Paso Robles, about halfway to its destination, Burke headed for the lavatory in the back of the plane, dropping the airbag on Thompson's lap as he passed. Moments later, Burke evidently shot his gun twice, killing Thompson.

"There's gunfire aboard!" yelled the pilot to air traffic controllers on the ground in Oakland. But on the voice recorder found in the wreckage of the plane was a much more insidious conversation, just after the sound of the cockpit door opening.

A female voice: "We have a problem."

The captain: "What kind of problem?"

Burke: "I'm the problem."

Two shots can be heard. The plane sped up and nosedived. A final shot sounded as Burke shot himself. The plane reached a speed of Mach 1.2 before breaking apart at 13,000 feet, its pieces scattered over a farm in Cayucos, along the Pacific Coast. All thirty-eight passengers and five crewmembers died.

Detective Bill Wammock of the San Luis Obispo County Sheriff's Office arrived first at the scene of a reported crash. He saw "nothing that resembled an airliner." For the first few hours, the sheriffs thought they were looking at a crash of a small plane. "We saw no pieces of the aircraft that were larger than, maybe, a human hand. It did not look like a passenger craft."

On the second day of searching the wreckage, federal investigators found a miniscule piece of skin on the trigger of a gun. The skin print matched David Burke. Also, they found the airbag with the handwritten note, six expended cartridges, and, eventually, the all-telling voice recorder.

The National Air Traffic Safety Board noted in its report that the cockpit doors were not bulletproof, which already was the standard on most foreign airlines. And it noted that David Burke had bypassed the metal detectors and screeners at the gate because he had used his US Air identification. While the FAA did not change the rule on cockpit doors, which later may have played a part in the 2001 World Trade Center and Pentagon crashes, rules were changed to require that all persons, including airline and airport employees, pass through the screening equipment.

Within four months PSA was gone, absorbed into the US Air fleet. The old "PSA expressway" from Los Angeles International Airport to San Francisco International Airport became a victim of corporate disinterest. "The Friendliest Airline" was lost forever, although for a time afterward, ex-PSA mechanics working for the new parent company would surreptitiously paint a friendly smile, just as a reminder of happier days.

CHAPTER 13

The Longest Minute
SYLMAR EARTHQUAKE
- 1971 -

LOS ANGELES MAY BE THE HOME OF EARTH-SHAKING blockbusters, but on Tuesday, February 9, 1971, Los Angeles shook itself awake when a quake hit about 25 miles north of downtown. At 6:02 A.M., just as many were rising to a new day, a series of jolts and shakes lasting over one minute rattled Southern California. Registering at magnitude 6.6 on the Richter scale, the temblor was the strongest within 100 miles of the city since records were kept.

Elevated freeways could not withstand the force generated by the earthquake.
Governor's Office of Emergency Services

The temblor was felt lightly in Los Angeles and Santa Ana but strongly as far away as Ventura, along the Pacific coast 90 miles north of downtown Los Angeles, and San Bernadino, about the same distance east of Los Angeles. It also was felt southward as far as San Diego.

The epicenter of the quake was said to be deep beneath the corner of Kenya Street and Wilbur Avenue in Northridge, a suburb of Los Angeles in the San Fernando Valley and future site of the worst earthquake in L.A. history (1994). Geological studies place it in the vicinity of Magic Mountain, a major amusement park in the area. But early damage reports centered on the collapse of the Olive View Medical Center in Sylmar, at the foot of the San Gabriel Mountains. Hence the earthquake was referred to as Sylmar by local and national media.

Seismologists call it the San Fernando earthquake, after the fault zone that caused it. The San Andreas Fault, which runs to the north and east of the San Gabriels, up to that point had been the focus of Southern California earthquake planning. Although the San Andreas did not move, the San Fernando quake helped to release some of the compression that occurs at a bend in the fault's path. In this case, to get around the bend in its road, the plate overthrusted, forcing the mountains to rise several feet. The area had been relatively quiet since a huge earthquake struck in 1593 about 5 miles from the 1971 quake. Most of the fault zone was still unmapped at the time of the Sylmar temblor.

Damage was found throughout the San Fernando Valley area. Communications were disrupted in this period before the advent of cellular telephones, as were water, gas, and electricity service, typical of earthquake scenarios. More than $500 million in losses to property occurred. In L.A. comedy circles they say timing is everything, and in this tragedy timing indeed was key to a rather small death toll of sixty-five, with one thousand injured. An hour later would have seen hundreds of thousands of commuters on the roads heading to work.

A shake two seconds longer in duration, it is estimated, would have emptied reservoirs onto unsuspecting residents living below them. Write that in a movie, and the audiences would have marveled at the serendipitous plot; in real life it was no laughing matter.

With an epicenter near the mountains, the danger of landslides of the hills appeared greatest. But when the areas most affected were determined to be away from urban areas, the focus of concern centered on three hospitals in the Sylmar area, the precarious proximity of a nearby dam, and the road damage on the freeways, the aortic streams of L.A. life.

The greatest loss of life occurred at the Veterans Administration Hospital in San Fernando. There, forty-nine people died as two buildings collapsed. Both buildings were about forty years old, built prior to the existence of more stringent earthquake codes and made of unreinforced masonry.

Three lives were lost as a result of the collapse of the Olive View Hospital buildings in Sylmar, the first reported damage. But the relatively low death toll should be seen as a triumph for a remarkable group of men and women who risked their lives to save their patients. The structures had been built to the level of earthquake safety of the code in place at that time. The code's levels just weren't good enough to withstand the duration of the shaking that the building endured. In one two-story building, the second floor pancaked, falling onto the first floor. Fortunately, no one was on the first floor at the time. Several stairwells, built as separate wings to the tallest building, pulled away from the structure.

During that violent minute, and in the several minutes that followed, 615 patients and 300 staff members made their way out of the buildings to safety. Two patients who relied on positive breathing apparatuses for their lives died without that life support; one staff member was hit by falling debris outside the hospital and died. Some of the other buildings on the hospital grounds were total losses.

In total, more than 1,700 mobile homes and 1,300 buildings throughout the area suffered major damage. But overall, recently built structures survived with little or no damage reported. Throughout, the greatest harm was done to those buildings constructed of unreinforced masonry, concrete without the added strength of a steel rebar. Had people been walking by such buildings when the quake hit—perhaps during the lunch or rush hours—who knows how many might have been hurt by flying bricks.

Most of the freeway damage occurred on the Golden State Freeway (I–5), which collapsed at the San Diego (I–405) and Santa Monica (I–210) interchanges and had rock slides in the Pacoima area. Two people died when another I–5 overpass collapsed at the Antelope Valley Freeway (SR–14). The Garden Grove Freeway developed cracks south of the San Diego Freeway.

The greatest threat to safety came at the Lower Van Norman dam in Mission Hills. This fifty-year-old, earth-filled concrete dam held an estimated six billion gallons of water, at the time the largest reservoir in the city system. A 60-foot section of the dam's southern edge had collapsed, and an 80-square-mile section of the valley was in danger. The concrete facing had crumbled, but the earthfill held the water from flooding. Later, after the draining of the lake, damage was found at both the lower and the upper dams, and they had to be replaced. More than 80,000 people were away from their homes for four days.

Seismologists and urban planners gained significant knowledge from this temblor. This region's planning had been predicated on movement along the San Andreas Fault, not on the largely unmapped nearby San Fernando fault zone. Many changes were made after this earthquake showed how important proper codes and their enforcement were to the safety and economic stability of the state. Building codes and requirements for freeways were strengthened for new construction. But, as we will see with regard to the Loma Prieta earthquake of 1989, the lack of retrofitting (strengthening of existing structures) left the Bay Area open to tragedy.

CHAPTER 14
We've Been Hit
MAJOR AIRLINE COLLISIONS
- 1971, 1978, and 1986 -

HUGHES AIR WEST FLIGHT 706 LOS ANGELES TO SALT LAKE CITY, UTAH. U.S. MARINE CORPS F-4B. June 6, 1971, was a typical hazy day in Los Angeles, scattered clouds with a 3-mile to 6-mile visibility. The yellow Hughes Air West DC-9, the "Flying Banana" as it was known, Flight 706, took off to fly to Salt Lake City, Utah, the first leg of six that would eventually take it to Seattle, Washington. The colorful Howard Hughes had decided to get back into the airline business and had bought Air West just the year before.

Photographer Hans Wendt was in the neighborhood as a burning Flight 182 headed toward a San Diego city block. ©1978 Hans Wendt

Two days before, on June 4, two US Marine Corps F-4B jet fighters left the Marine Corps Air Station (MCAS) in El Toro, California, on an overnight flight to McCord Air Force Base in Washington, D.C., with a return scheduled for the next day. The planes developed problems from the outset, starting with their transponders. They proceeded to McCord under control of the air traffic controllers, but then one lost radio contact. Both landed safely.

On June 5, they headed back and made it to Mountain Home Air Force Base in Idaho, where they developed oxygen leaks and radar degradation. The mechanics at Mountain Home were unable to get the transponders to work, but they did replace a burned fuse to fix the radio. Because of the need for repairs, the planes then headed to Naval Auxiliary Air Station in Fallon, Nevada, where they hoped to get the problems fixed.

When Fallon was unable to fix them, the crew consulted the squadron duty officer for instructions. They were commanded to return to MCAS El Toro at low altitude. However, they could not depart until an air show at the air base was completed. They departed on June 6 at 5:14 P.M.

They flew at varying altitudes over the Sierra Nevada Mountains until they were over Bakersfield, where they changed flight course to avoid heavy traffic out of Los Angeles, flying east of Palmdale at 1,000 feet minimum. But the visibility deteriorated at that level, and they rose to 15,500 feet. They leveled off 50 miles away from El Toro.

According to the testimony of the radio interception officer (RIO), at this point the pilot of one of the aircraft executed a barrel roll, a 360-degree aileron roll that took three seconds to complete. Moving at 420 knots and using a degraded radar system, the RIO saw no other aircraft on his screen, but then he caught sight of the DC-9 and shouted to the pilot, who had already started evasive maneuvers. They were not successful.

The collision took place near Duarte, a town at the foot of the

San Gabriel Mountains, not far from the epicenter of the San Fernando earthquake earlier that year. The wreckage was found in two canyons in the mountains. All the passengers and crew of the DC-9, a total of 49, and one crew member of the F-4B died. One crew member ejected successfully.

In its report the National Transportation Safety Board (NTSB) observed that three separate radar systems failed to show the F-4B as a potential threat to the DC-9, a limitation of the systems themselves. And it also noted that the pilot of the Marine fighter jet failed to request traffic advisories, which would have alerted controllers to the plane being in the area, and, by choosing to go around Los Angeles, the plane had to pass through the area that eastbound traffic ordinarily travels at an hour when travel was heavy. Furthermore, at the pilot's command, the RIO was radar mapping in a heavily trafficked area; a second set of eyes outward would have helped.

PSA FLIGHT 182 — SACRAMENTO TO SAN DIEGO CESSNA TRAINING PLANE. Mervin Dymally, lieutenant governor of the state of California, looked at his calendar for September 25, 1978, and decided that he was overbooked. Expected in Southern California later in the day, he had to make a choice about which flight he would take to San Diego. He decided that, rather than take the early morning flight down, he would fly in the night before, moving him off of PSA Flight 182. That decision saved his life.

On September 25, Hans Wendt, a photographer for San Diego County, was taking photographs of new gas station recovery-nozzle pumping devices on University Avenue in San Diego. Hearing a loud thump, he looked up; with his photographic training guiding him, Wendt took two photos of a Boeing 727 with its right wing flaming as it dove into a nearby neighborhood.

People living near the corner of Dwight and Nile Streets didn't know what was about to hit them. Tons of steel, along with fragments of plastic, fabric, and human beings, descended at more than 300 miles an hour into their homes, destroying a city block.

The sky was clear with visibility at 10 miles, according to the records of the National Transportation Safety Board. A Cessna 172 training plane had taken off from San Diego's Lindbergh Field on a northeasterly heading, preparing to do instrument-landing approaches with aborts on Runway 9. It was in contact with the San Diego Approach Control.

PSA Flight 182 had left Sacramento and landed at Los Angeles International Airport (LAX) to deplane and board passengers en route to San Diego. Taking off from LAX, the plane made contact with San Diego Approach Control. The crew was told to use Runway 27 and switched to Lindbergh Control Tower, which put them on visual flight rules. The controller told them about a Cessna 172 and gave them headings to its location. The pilot verified that they saw the small plane. The pilot was to keep the Cessna in visual separation, meaning that as long as he could see it maintaining separation, he could continue the approach for landing. The rules delineate that the pilot is to inform the tower whenever he loses sight of the other aircraft. The crew of the PSA plane confirmed seeing the Cessna.

After two practice runs, the instructor on the Cessna decided on a third, and the plane pulled up for a climbout to the northeast. Lindbergh Tower set a northeast heading of 070 with visual flight rules in effect. The Cessna confirmed and repeated the heading. Later it would be determined that the plane moved to a 090 degree heading, the same as the bigger jet, without informing the control tower.

Flight 182 turned onto its downwind leg and was advised of the Cessna's position. Looking around, the captain and first officer discovered that the smaller plane was not in sight.

   8:59:28 Captain to control tower: "We're looking."
   9:00:41 Captain: "Is that the one [we're] looking at?"

	Copilot: "Yeah, but I don't see him now."
9:00:44	Captain: "Okay, we had it there a minute ago."
9:00:50	Captain: "I think he's passed off to our right."
9:00:52	Captain: "He was right over there a minute ago."
9:01:11	First officer: "Are we clear of that Cessna?"
	Flight engineer: "Supposed to be."
9:01:21	Captain: "Oh yeah, before we turned downwind, I saw him about one o'clock, probably behind us now."

Thinking they had passed it, the pilots continued the larger jet's approach.

At 9:01:28, the conflict alert warning suddenly alarmed at the San Diego Approach Control Facility. The alert system monitors all flights and predicts their trajectories. When it predicts a possible collision, it sets off a warning. The system was only in place for about six weeks, and there had been an average of thirteen alerts per day, many of which were false.

At 9:01:47, the air controller said "Traffic in your vicinity" to the Cessna pilot, who was in voice contact with San Diego Approach. At 9:01:47.9, the two aircraft collided at 2,600 feet altitude.

Eyewitnesses testified that PSA 182 banked slightly and the Cessna pitched nose up, colliding with the right wing of the bigger plane. Fire shot out from the damaged wing and increased its descent. The Cessna was destroyed.

Flight 182 crashed into the North Park neighborhood, 3 miles from Lindbergh Field, at 9:02:07. All 136 passengers and seven crew onboard the flight died. Both the instructor and the student in the Cessna died. Nine people on the ground died. Twenty-two homes were destroyed or damaged. It was, to that time, the worst aircraft disaster in U.S. history.

The NTSB's findings placed the responsibility for the accident on the PSA flight crew. Even though the Cessna had veered off its course of 070 degrees to 090 and hadn't reported the change to air traffic control, the larger plane was the overtaking flight and had not maintained the necessary separation, according to the rules.

The findings also looked closely at the responsibility of the air traffic controller, who had nineteen seconds from alert to collision to have contacted the Cessna or the Boeing jet. They concluded that the controller was misled by the belief that the Boeing knew where the Cessna was and was separating, as well as the knowledge that there had been several false alarms each day. The lack of a requirement in the rules to notify the pilots of the planes of a possible danger contributed to the resulting collision by not giving the pilots an opportunity to respond.

AEROMEXICO FLIGHT 498 MEXICO CITY TO LOS ANGELES PIPER PA-28-181 ARCHER AIRCRAFT. William Kramer, his wife, and one of their daughters set out from Torrance Airport in their Piper aircraft for an excursion to Big Bear Lake in the San Bernadino Mountains. The skies were clear on that Sunday, August 31, 1986, as they traveled eastward.

Aeromexico Flight 498, a Douglas DC-9-32 jetliner, had left Mexico City that same morning and, after stops in Guadalajara, Loreto, and Tijuana, was about to finish its last leg, on landing approach to Los Angeles International Airport. A crew of six was responsible for the safety and comfort of the fifty-eight passengers on board.

The Piper strayed off its path and entered Los Angeles's Terminal Control Area (TCA). It failed to make contact with air traffic controllers, and, while its transponder was working, the controller failed to pick up the unidentified aircraft on his screen.

Controller Walter R. C. White, at that time, was having some problems with another private aircraft, a Grumman Yankee, that had violated the TCA. He had a few exchanges with the pilot about being in the middle of the TCA where jets run through (in fact the controller told the Grumman that the plane just missed being hit by one of those jets); meanwhile the Piper kept moving farther into another part of the airspace. It may have been this distraction that kept the controller from noticing the Piper, or it may have been flaws in the FAA tracking system, which had blind spots in the area the Piper was flying. Either way, the controller did not see the Piper on his screen.

At 11:52:36 A.M., the controller noticed that the computer was no longer tracking Flight 498, and he notified the arrival coordinator of the loss of contact—both radar and radio. He'd lost contact because at 11:52:09 A.M., at an altitude of 6,560 feet over the city of Cerritos, the Piper hit the tail of the bigger jet. Both planes crashed—the Piper into an empty schoolyard, the DC-9 into a residential block, destroying or damaging a dozen houses. All sixty-four people on the Aeromexico flight, all three people on the Piper, and fifteen people on the ground were killed. This accident was the worst air disaster to that time in California.

In the investigation the National Transportation Safety Board (NTSB) interviewed many of the people who had taught William Kramer to fly or had flown with him. He was seen as conscientious and careful. One friend even declared he was "too careful" with pre-flight readiness.

The possibility was raised that William Kramer might have had a heart attack before the collision, according to the pathologist who testified at a later civil trial. If that were the case, did the Piper stray into restricted airspace because the family was trying to overcome an emergency situation? The NTSB determined that there was no infarction (heart attack) discovered in the autopsy. The fact that the passengers were all wearing seat belts when found indicated that they were not performing emergency aid, and the data showed that the plane climbed steadily, banking 5 percent at one point before the collision, indicating the actions of a conscious and alert pilot.

The NTSB held that the collision was caused by flaws in the radar-tracking system and in procedures in use at the time. It also faulted the Piper for its incursion into restricted airspace. It recommended the certification of the Traffic Alert and Collision Avoidance System, the requirement of compatible equipment on all planes, better enforcement of the "see and avoid" procedures, and punitive measures against aircraft that fly in restricted space without permission.

Nearly one hundred civil suits were filed against the airlines, the controller and the FAA. The FAA blamed the two pilots of the planes, while Aeromexico faulted Kramer and the FAA. The families of the crash victims blamed the air traffic controller.

The controller testified that he never saw the Piper on his screen. The crash victims' families hired an expert to recreate the radar screen from data recorded at the air traffic control center, which showed that the Piper was definitely on the screen.

The jury in the civil suit returned a verdict holding the United States government (the FAA) 50 percent responsible and William Kramer 50 percent responsible for the accident. A total of $56.5 million was paid to the families. While the largest single payment was for $5.6 million, many settled for 10 percent of that and have carried their bitterness over the years.

Many changes have been made, but the real problem rests in the ever-increasing number of flights in the L.A. area from too many airports. Even with the installation of better equipment using better technology, and with tightened enforcement of the rules, accidents happen.

CHAPTER 15
World Series Earthquake
LOMA PRIETA
- 1989 -

AMERICAN TELEVISION VIEWERS AND BASEBALL FANS got all shook up on Tuesday, October 17, 1989. At 5:04 P.M. Pacific daylight time—just as the starting pitchers of the third game of the World Series were beginning their warm-ups and lineup cards were about to be exchanged at home plate at Candlestick Park, home of the San Francisco Giants—the stadium, with more than half of its expected crowd of 70,000 already in their seats, shook. The shaking lasted fifteen seconds, with people holding on for their lives.

Support pillars protrude through the southbound lanes as Highway 1 near Watsonville drops to the ground. Governor's Office of Emergency Services

Concrete on the upper deck of the structure cracked. When at last the shaking stopped, the World Series, the Bay Area, indeed, the Central Coast of California as far away as Monterey, were left in turmoil.

No one in the stadium knew exactly what to do. Was it really over, or was this just the first of many temblors? Could the game between the Giants and the Oakland A's proceed, even without electricity? Were the people in the park safer in the stands than out on the freeways? Just how bad was this quake?

Rumors abounded. Some said that San Francisco was on fire and on the verge of destruction. The Bay Bridge, said others, had fallen down. Black smoke could be seen from the upper decks of the stadium. Power and telephone communications were out throughout the area, and in those years before the proliferation of cell phones, few could make calls to loved ones to let them know they were all right.

Park and baseball officials realized that they needed to cancel the game and help make sure that those in the stands were safe and felt safe. For the next few hours, baseball was replaced with fear.

The epicenter of the earthquake was in the Santa Cruz Mountains under Mt. Loma Prieta, about 5 miles north of the entrance to Nisene Marks State Park in Aptos, a town about 8 miles south of Santa Cruz. Ironically, Loma Prieta, which ominously means "dark mountain" in Spanish, had been the site of the greatest loss of forest land in the San Francisco Earthquake in 1906.

This quake, now named Loma Prieta, was measured at first at 6.9 on the Richter scale, but then was upgraded to 7.1. Ten years after the quake, it was downgraded to 6.9 again. Tremors were felt as far away as Reno in the east and Los Angeles to the south. A 4-foot tsunami developed in Monterey Bay, with water sucked from the shore at Santa Cruz taking twenty minutes to crash on the beaches in Monterey. A major landslide occurred underwater in Monterey Bay.

In the Marina District in the northwest part of San Francisco, damage was the heaviest because the area was built on landfill; part of that landfill was the debris from the 1906 earthquake and fire, and part was from a swampy area that had been filled in for the 1915 San Francisco Panama-Pacific International Exposition, which had been held to celebrate the comeback of the city from its devastation. Here, with no foundation to the land, the houses and buildings toppled or were so badly damaged that some residents later would be given only fifteen minutes to go back in to get their possessions before the buildings were demolished.

Just as in 1906, gas lines and water mains broke, starting fires and making firefighting difficult. Bucket brigades moved water to fight many of the twenty-seven fires throughout the city. Again, the worst fires were in the Marina District. The city's emergency telephone systems failed when a fire broke out in the equipment room of the 911 headquarters, so fire alarms were used to summon emergency workers until the 911 system was repaired.

The world focused on the major road calamities: the San Francisco-Oakland Bay Bridge closing, the collapse of the Cypress Freeway (I–880) upper deck in Oakland, and the destruction of the Embarcadero Freeway in San Francisco. Ordinarily, with that much damage to major roadways during evening commute, hundreds if not thousands might have lost their lives. But the World Series, which featured both Bay Area baseball teams, had many fans starting for home earlier than usual, making traffic light for that hour. To the credit of the officials in Oakland, their refusal to speculate about the number of deaths kept panic from setting in. And, while there are tragic stories of loss in the rubble of the Cypress, relatively few—forty-two—died. Throughout the earthquake zone from the Monterey Peninsula to the north coast, only sixty-two people lost their lives. More than 3,000 were injured, and more than 8,000 were left homeless.

Perhaps the most televised and dramatic rescue was that of Julio Berumen, a six-year-old boy trapped in the steel and concrete collapse of the freeway, his mother and friends dead in the car with him.

Dr. James Betts, brought to the scene to help, performed an amputation on the boy's leg that saved his life; to do so the rescue team had to saw in half his dead friend in the seat next to him.

The Bay Bridge shook violently during the temblor, and a section of its upper deck collapsed onto the deck below. The bridge had been designed to protect it from collapsing completely, to have sections give way to release pressure on the whole structure. Miraculously, only one person died in the collapse.

But the temporary loss of the bridge placed tremendous burdens upon public transportation. Bay Area Rapid Transit (BART), the commuter train line connecting communities around the San Francisco Bay, saw a 50 percent increase in ridership. A commuter ferry system was established to points in the East Bay. Southern Pacific set up ferries from East Bay and North Bay points to ferry freight into and out of the city.

Fortunately, Interstate 580, which had been in construction for several years between Berkeley and the Richmond-San Raphael Bridge, was close to completion. Construction crews working around the clock finished the road and opened it in just a few days, allowing auto commuters a faster route to the bridge to Marin County, from which they could then drive south to the Golden Gate Bridge to get to the city.

But the Embarcadero Freeway, within the city, was crippled badly and, even though repairable, was abandoned. Considered an eyesore by many locals, the city eventually chose to tear it down and replace it with a ground-level boulevard. Part of the Central Freeway was also damaged, and parts of it were removed as well; a boulevard is planned.

But the eastern span of the Bay Bridge was only repaired. Fights over design plans for a new span and rising costs of materials have gone on almost since the day of the collapse. Local governments and regional agencies continue to clash with the state over what the span will look like and who will pay for it. Every day that passes brings another earthquake closer without a safe bridge on which to travel between San Francisco and Oakland.

Both San Francisco and Oakland experienced significant damage to their city halls. Oakland saw many of its older downtown buildings damaged. Both cities have redesigned and remodeled their centers of government, and Oakland developers replaced or rebuilt other buildings in the inner city.

Other parts of the Bay Area also suffered. Nearly a million books fell off the shelves in Clark Library at San Jose State University, while one of the Stanford University libraries was so badly damaged it was closed for years. The Burlingame Hyatt, near the San Francisco airport, a year old at the time and built to the latest in earthquake safety codes, suffered significant structural damage ($8 million). On Interstate 280 the motion was so violent that sections of the road slammed into one another, fracturing columns and breaking off concrete leaving the reinforced steel of the pillars exposed.

Santa Cruz County Shakes the Worst

The world's attention was on the San Francisco Bay Area because the collapse of freeways and bridges affected so many commuters, but the quake struck at the heart and soul of two towns in Santa Cruz County, 75 miles south of San Francisco. The city of Santa Cruz, at that time with a population of about 50,000, was (and is) a tourist and college town situated at the northern tip of Monterey Bay. A vibrant city, with shops, restaurants, bookstores, and boutique businesses along its main business district, Pacific Avenue, Santa Cruz thrived during the academic year as approximately 8,000 students attended the University of California on the hill overlooking town. As with many American cities, however, major businesses had moved to malls on the city's outskirts, leaving vacant storefronts downtown, where aging buildings bordered on neglect. During the summer months hordes of tourists come to Santa Cruz to enjoy its beach and boardwalk area and to walk

Downtown Santa Cruz after the 1989 Loma Prieta earthquake. Governor's Office of Emergency Services

its municipal wharf, which offers seafood restaurants and tourist shops. (Recent figures show that 3.5 million people come to the beach/boardwalk and wharf each year.)

Watsonville, about 15 miles south of Santa Cruz along Highway 1, was even closer to the epicenter. In 1989 it was primarily an agricultural town of about 30,000 people, many of whom were poor. Canneries and frozen-food processing plants had closed, causing the loss of many jobs. Meanwhile, seasonal and permanent agricultural fieldwork increased. And the city lost retail tax income from the flight of stores to malls in other towns and counties.

The number of houses destroyed in a matter of fifteen seconds was staggering to a city the size of Watsonville: 237 destroyed and 405 damaged. Thousands of people were suddenly homeless and had to join a great tent city set up to temporarily house those without shelter. The last remaining department store collapsed, as did the Odd Fellows building they were two of the oldest structures in town. Businesses, which had been suffering from the high unemployment rate before the quake, closed up shop for good. Highway 1, the connection to Monterey, became impassable.

In Santa Cruz the quake's proximity intensified the seismic wave action, bringing down many of the older buildings on Pacific Avenue, while damaging structures throughout the city. The only direct route to nearby San Jose, Highway 17—a winding four-lane commuter highway through the mountains—was closed by a landslide caused by the quake. With power out, communications out, houses and buildings destroyed, many local roads impassable, and its highway lifeline shut down, the people of Santa Cruz faced the shock of a destroyed city and limited physical help in the first days after the temblor. For the most part, they were on their own.

The smell of leaking gas and sewage was what many county residents talked about in the days after the quake. These lines, along with water mains, had broken all over both cities and throughout the county. Hundreds of houses, especially in the Santa Cruz Mountains along the San Andreas Fault, were thrown off their foundations or collapsed from landslides or earth movement.

The city and county had suffered from disasters before: In 1955 downtown was flooded with nearly a foot of water, and in 1982 18 inches of rain fell in the watershed in one day, causing floods in the mountains and loss of homes. The flooded San Lorenzo River took down a vital bridge in town, severing communications and electricity lines for tens of thousands of people for days. The lessons learned from those emergencies had given the city and the county of Santa Cruz an edge in this latest calamity. And while there were problems in communications and in response, overall city and county services in this small town and region worked well to provide safety and essential services in crisis.

The loss in dollars would come to about $1 billion; the cost in lives, homes, and emotional stability for those who survived was, to paraphrase a commercial, priceless. Without electricity, structurally sound homes, and functioning businesses, the displaced waited for help—a place to sleep, food to eat, and basic and urgent medical care.

In the city of Santa Cruz, emergency workers cordoned off the downtown area, displacing hundreds—many elderly, who lived in the two residential hotels on Pacific Avenue—and closing all of the businesses in the area. Buildings needed to be inspected for structural soundness, and those who lived or worked in these businesses, once safety was determined, were given fifteen minutes to enter—escorted—to retrieve their possessions.

In those first few days, tensions between emergency workers and locals were high; people showed their upset at nature's wrath by directing their anger toward those who were making critical decisions that affected the search for earthquake victims who might still be alive. And in the middle of this crisis, the president of the United States invited himself to see the damage. For several hours before his arrival, the Secret Service stopped all search and rescue activities in the areas that the president would be visiting, threatening the lives of those still trapped in the teetering buildings.

Within days 470,000 square feet of building space was gone, demolished and removed by truck, leaving gaping holes surrounded by chain-link fence. Included in the demolition was the Cooper House, a century-old structure, once the county's headquarters, that had become the central meeting place in downtown. Inside this building were stores, offices, and restaurants. Outside, on certain afternoons most of the year, crowds had gathered to listen to the sounds of reggae or rock performed by local groups at an outdoor cafe. This particular loss, along with the destruction of the beloved Book Shop Santa Cruz and surrounding coffeehouses and retail shops, brought home to many residents the seriousness of the task that lay in front of them.

Planning Recovery

Local businesses, residents, labor unions, and city agencies came together in those first few days to create temporary quarters for downtown businesses. By erecting huge circus-size canvas tents—later known as the Phoenix Pavilions—and trailers, some of the businesses reopened to the slogan "Shop local." The inventory of Book Shop Santa Cruz was saved by 400 volunteers who went into the damaged building. Little did they know that they would be in those makeshift buildings for as much as three years as the downtown was replanned and reconstructed.

The ironies of the politics of the city were great. Businesses that had been renting downtown space in buildings often neglected by their owners had to wait for the owners to rebuild the buildings. Changing demographics had brought about a change in city government about a decade before, so now a progressive, antigrowth city council faced the daunting task of envisioning and implementing a plan for the future economic recovery of downtown. The building and property owners, without a guarantee of tenants, had to figure out a way to convince local, regional, and national commercial investors to trust in a revitalization program of immense proportions. And key to this revitalization program was that all members of the community, regardless of political persuasion or economic class, had to be heard and their valid ideas worked into a viable plan. Vision Santa Cruz, a group of about thirty-six leaders from all parts of the community, developed such a plan in a sometimes acrimonious but most-times cooperative atmosphere. Thousands of hours were put into developing a plan that created a mix of entertainment and dining venues, offices, and shops with affordable and luxury housing, while attempting to maintain the charm of the old Santa Cruz downtown.

Recovery has taken more than a decade and a half. Two properties on the avenue are still fenced holes, but downtown Santa Cruz is a destination for residents and tourists alike. Sleepy Santa Cruz, where

Downtown Watsonville was devastated by the Loma Prieta earthquake. Governor's Office of Emergency Services

there was little to do at night besides movies and coffeehouses, has been reenergized. A viable nightlife of clubs, theaters, and dining is enhanced by the city's event promotions and street festivals. And while the politics of the city are no less contentious than before the earthquake, sworn enemies have found ways to work together—if not always, then often enough.

In Watsonville there is also a new downtown brought about by the destruction of the earthquake of 1989. Revitalization has included a new department store, about 150,000 square feet of retail space, the development of a Watsonville branch of the mid-county Cabrillo College, the rebuilding of several buildings, the refurbishing of Watsonville High School, and the opening of the Mello Center for the Performing Arts. Hundreds of new homes, many through affordable-housing programs, have been built or are in the planning stages, and 300,000 square feet of retail space has been added outside of downtown, with more coming.

The most critical change that has occurred for the state of California is a new understanding of the need for a unified and standardized plan of action in emergencies. Today, local, county, regional, and state agencies and governments are able to communicate and coordinate with each other as never before. State standards have been drawn up so that the equipment of one agency will be compatible with equipment from another, allowing a neighboring city or county to send equipment and personnel that can easily work in aiding the effort of a victim city.

The lessons of the Loma Prieta earthquake do not end there. Studies have shown that this quake did not occur on the San Andreas Fault, where one tectonic plate carrying the coastline meets another plate that carries the mainland. It occurred on a secondary fault nearby. The lesson of Loma Prieta is that we haven't seen anything so far. The big one has yet to come.

CHAPTER 16
Poisoning the Sacramento
DUNSMUIR TOXIC SPILL
- 1991 -

> BEST WATER ON EARTH
> —Sign at the railroad junction in Dunsmuir

CALIFORNIANS KNEW FEW PLACES AS BEAUTIFUL AND serene as the pristine waters of the Upper Sacramento River. The river teemed with thousands of trout and other fish from the Box Canyon Dam to Shasta Lake, a distance of about 45 miles. The fish,

Aerial view of emergency vehicles after an overturned tanker leaked 19,000 gallons of a deadly herbicide into the Sacramento River. Governor's Office of Emergency Services

mostly trout, feasted on the multitude of insects that hover near the surface of the water, making it easy and fun for vacationers to fish and catch. Nearby is Mount Shasta, one of California's mighty peaks, snow-covered in winter and a hiker's dream the rest of the year.

In the town of Dunsmuir, situated along the river about 38 miles north of the lake, is a strategic junction in the myriad of railroad tracks owned by Southern Pacific. Just north of town, as the tracks approach and cross the Sacramento River, trains slow to a crawl as they take a 180-degree hairpin curve known as the Cantara Loop.

The successful movement through this loop and on down the 2 percent grade of the Sacramento River depends on the smooth, steady push that keeps a train on its tracks. Southern Pacific had a policy of oiling its tracks to keep down friction that causes wear and tear. But oil creates slippage of the wheels against the tracks, and that causes dangerous and uncontrollable lateral movement of the cars. But on this particular day, there were other problems with a ninety-seven-car train negotiating the Loop. According to reports, two of the four engines of the train had mechanical defects. The cars were improperly weighted, with heavy cars interspersed among empties, instead of the empty cars being placed at the rear.

Twice the engineer, feeling the wheels slip, added sand to cut down on the slippage. But then the engines surged, and the last engine and seven cars derailed, hanging precariously over the river. An unmarked tanker fell into the water. It was 9:50 P.M. on Sunday, July 14, 1991.

It wasn't the first derailment near or on the Loop (there had been forty-one in the preceding fifteen years), nor will it be the last (in 1997, 2 miles from the Cantara Loop, another train derailed, sending five cars into the river—fortunately, only traces of deadly chemicals leaked). But this time, that one car that landed in the river ruptured; the tanker, carrying a deadly herbicide, metam sodium, leaked 19,000 gallons of the poison into the waters, which headed downstream.

The manifest for the train didn't list the tanker's contents as hazardous, because the state of California, the U.S. Environmental Protection Agency, and the U.S. Department of Transportation did not classify metam sodium as a hazardous substance. But the odor itself smelled of poison so badly that the train's engineer and conductor radioed headquarters, uncoupled an engine, and rode away to safety.

Police and other law enforcement quickly realized the danger to the population and started to spread the word to stay away from the plume, to not eat anything from the river, and to "keep your windows up and drive like hell" on Interstate 5 where the freeway crosses the Sacramento. On Monday morning local residents along the river started to complain of dizziness, shortness of breath, headaches, vomiting, and other symptoms of poisoning. The emergency rooms filled quickly that day as the river's life through Dunsmuir quickly died.

By Tuesday morning the chemical had reached Castle Crags State Park. Authorities kept vacationers away from the river, monitoring the movement of the spill. Continuing at a slow pace, the metam sodium finally reached Shasta Lake, a body of freshwater created by Shasta Dam, on Wednesday. Ironically, the dam was responsible for the death of the local salmon population when the fish could no longer get to their spawning grounds.

From Dunsmuir to Shasta Lake, a distance of about 38 miles, not one animal or insect still lived in or around the water. Being an herbicide, the plants in and along the river also died. A complete ecosystem was destroyed.

In later reports the proper manner in which the Southern Pacific Railroad should have acted entailed immediately informing local and state authorities so that the Siskyou Dam, upstream from the spill, could close its gates to stop the flow of water into the river. That would have slowed the chemical flume from moving downstream. Then the railroad should have established another dammed area to catch the chemical and pump it out of the river. But according to all accounts, Southern Pacific did not report the problem until the next morning, and at that time was more concerned about getting the locomotive out of the river than sealing off the poison.

Over the next dozen years, Southern Pacific and then Union Pacific, which had bought its competitor in 1996, denied its culpability and fought to keep the state from enforcing safety regulations. Union Pacific also canceled Southern Pacific's promise to build a new bridge at Cantara Loop, instead finally agreeing to an upgrade of the track bed and a catch rail that runs parallel to the track.

Dunsmuir was financially devastated. Its very existence, from hardware stores to restaurants, from motels to campgrounds, was dependent on tourist fishing. The town had already been suffering from a lack of business due to the lack of snow from a five-year drought that kept skiers away. Successful trout seasons kept Dunsmuir going. And until July 14, business had been good. Suddenly, no one was coming to the area. Now it was no snow, no fish, no income.

The Department of Fish and Game proposed a recovery plan that allowed only catch-and-release provisions for the river and its tributaries, to the great anger of local merchants who wanted their fishing tourism back. The business owners suggested bringing in trout from fish hatcheries, but they were warned that without a food supply fish that were introduced would not survive except by forcing out the native fish that still populated nearby streams.

Surprisingly—since first estimates were that the river would not come back for decades—that October, the first signs of life returned to the river in the form of moss and algae. Then insects returned. And finally the native trout, which had indeed survived by hiding in the unscathed tributaries to the Upper Sacramento, came back. Within months much of the ecosystem had begun to rebuild itself. Certain indigenous species that were found only in the area have not reappeared, but otherwise a visitor in Dunsmuir today would never know that there had ever been such death and destruction.

Despite estimates that life wouldn't come back to the river for decades, nature showed signs of bouncing back in just three months.
Governor's Office of Emergency Services

    The irony is that Dunsmuir's sign at the entrance of town, THE WORLD'S BEST WATER, never referred to the Upper Sacramento River. Its water comes from Mossbrae Springs, unaffected by the river contamination.

    The Union Pacific Railroad has stated that it cannot promise that another derailment won't occur at the Cantera Loop, but they would catch the pollution before it gets into the river. Will the one guardrail in place be sufficient to hold back many tons of steel and chemical? Each day dangerous, toxic cargo passes this very spot, yet there are no new controls or new oversight of the workings of the railroads and the manner in which they transport these chemicals. Nature showed that it could withstand *this* chemical. But can it overcome all of them? Only time will tell.

CHAPTER 17

Burning Hills
OAKLAND TUNNEL FIRE
- 1991 -

THE BAY AREA HAD BEEN HAVING A TOUGH TIME BY 1991. A five-year drought had dried up foliage throughout the area; a devastating earthquake had destroyed freeways and buildings just two years before. And now, in October, usually a cool-weather month, the temperatures were hovering around ninety degrees.

In the Oakland hills homes with wood-shingled roofs often had been built on the steep hillsides to get a view of the bay; the rule of thumb was the more bridges you could see from your house, the

Firemen survey the damage caused by the Oakland Fire. Governor's Office of Emergency Services

greater your status and the more expensive the property. The homes were situated among huge eucalyptus and pine trees, and vegetation was thick, often right around the houses themselves. That past December, a freeze had killed a lot of the vegetation, leaving the dead plants to wilt and dry up. Homeowners had been warned to clear the brush, but few had heeded the alert. The fuel was waiting for the right conditions. And on October 20, 1991, the right conditions came together.

The day before had seen a brushfire on a six-acre parcel of land in the hills above the Berkeley-Oakland line, not far from Highway 24 and the Caldecott Tunnel. The Oakland Fire Department had put it out and, following standard procedure, left their hoses in place for the next morning when they would dowse hot spots that might still be burning. The fire was inspected during the night, and the crews came the next day to spray.

That October morning was extremely hot, and onshore winds with gusts up to sixty-five miles an hour brought the heat of the Central Valley to the coast. The firefighters found that grass and embers were burning on the acreage of the previous brushfire, and they hosed down the areas. In the midst of the hosing, eyewitnesses said they watched a single ember, caught by the strong winds, fly out of the burn area and land on a tree. The tree exploded! And so, at 10:58 A.M., the firestorm began.

The fire was out of control within moments. The winds moved more embers out to waiting dry wood. The fire spread in all directions, making the efforts of the twenty-five-person crew at the scene futile. Calls were immediately made for more trucks and equipment, but the fire took off. By noon, one hour later, almost 800 homes had been destroyed.

Homeowners were taken unawares and, startled by the sudden appearance of the fire, first rushed to hose down their rooftops and then fled for their lives. But when they got in their cars and tried to leave, they found their ways blocked on the narrow lanes that wound their way through the hills. With residents fleeing downhill and fire trucks climbing uphill, the impasse caused panic among the residents and hardships for the firefighters.

When the firefighters arrived from neighboring cities, their 2.5-inch hose connectors did not match the 3-inch Oakland hydrants. And when they did, there was little water to pump, because pressure was low from the loss of water from pipes that had burst from the intense heat of the burning houses.

While many residents fled, others stayed. They, along with the firefighters from several surrounding cities and student volunteers from the area, worked to stop the flames on the ground. But it soon became apparent that, with so much smoke being generated by the flames, no one was quite sure where to direct the action to be most effective. The cloud that was generated by the fire billowed black smoke for miles, the easterly winds taking most of it over the Golden Gate Bridge and out to the ocean. But on the ground, visibility was zero. There was no comprehensive picture of what they were fighting.

NASA-Ames Research Center sent in a high-altitude ER-2 Airborne Science aircraft and two C-130 transport planes to map the fire. Infrared video photographs of the entire region were taken by the ER-2, and the transports took infrared images and video footage. Infrared imaging can penetrate smoke. The data was then helicoptered to the command center, where it was overlaid on maps to determine where the fire was and where it seemed to be heading. This identification allowed the fire command to employ the firefighters in a more effective manner.

The California Division of Forestry sent fixed-wing aircraft and helicopters. Aerial fire fighting helped, although it was hampered by the concentration of the fire in a relatively small and steep space and by the fact that the area in flames was within the terminal control area for Oakland International Airport. Only two tankers could spray fire retardant on the flames at a time, and even then it was difficult for the planes to see where they were going. That limited their use. Meanwhile, helicopters, dipping their baskets into nearby lakes and adding retardant foam as they flew back to the fire, were able to drop smaller and less-effective amounts on the fire. The hope was to retard the fire enough to hold the perimeter until a change in the weather—especially the winds—took place.

Firefighters also were hampered by the lack of a good communications system. Airwaves were too limited for the number of units at work and the four division field commands. Additionally, the hills themselves hindered the signal. One of the changes Oakland made after the fire was to develop a system that could be used in hilly terrain.

Meanwhile the wind was creating havoc in Oakland and alarming residents as far away as San Francisco. Burning embers from exploding trees and houses were picked up by the winds and sent south and east, landing on buildings throughout San Francisco. And the fire itself, in need of oxygen as well as fuel, sucked the air in, creating a swirling effect even as the larger winds slowed. And finally, the intensity of the firestorm actually created a water-vapor cloud right above itself, when otherwise there were no clouds on this hot, sunny day anywhere in the Bay Area.

Remarkable stories of the speed and wrath of the fire abound. In a matter of moments, a peaceful morning was turned into a fiery hell. Most witnesses said there was no time to gather anything but themselves. In one story, a man sent his wife and mother in the car and went back in to gather a few possessions. He hopped on his motorcycle and fled as the house was nearly surrounded by the flames. With no place to go but through the flames, he gunned his cycle and charged ahead. He made it through, with about 20 percent of his body burned. A group of firefighters near Grizzly Peak was trapped; they hosed themselves down, lay down, and waited as the firestorm swept over them. Only one of the crew was burned severely.

Fireplaces and gates left standing. Governor's Office of Emergency Services

Finally, in the late afternoon the winds died down and changed direction, pushing the fire back upon itself in the already burned area, now 1,500 acres in a 5.25-mile perimeter. This allowed the firefighters to cordon off the fire, and they were able to hold the perimeter until the fire was out, officially, on the fourth day. In the end more than 3,000 homes were burned and 5,000 people were left homeless. Twenty-six people lost their lives. Total damages were $1.5 billion. It was the worst wildfire in California history, and one of the worst in the history of the nation.

With the fire over the search for the bodies of those unaccounted for began. Using dogs and sifting equipment, bones were collected and identified. The area was guarded against looting. Just as a tornado can cause great destruction and yet leave unharmed objects in its path, so did this storm of fire. With houses burned to their foundations, some recently planted trees and grass survived. A house might be destroyed, but a Halloween pumpkin sat unharmed.

Insurance adjusters began to estimate individual damage costs. The city of Oakland established a central office near the fire area to assist homeowners in the building-permit process. Within six months the first house was rebuilt. Thousands more have been rebuilt since.

Some changes were made to help to protect against another fire in the hills of Oakland. The picturesque lanes have been widened to allow two vehicles to pass. Trees have been replanted, but much farther from homes than before. Tile has replaced wood as the roof shingle of choice in the area.

But evidence of the fire remains, certainly in the higher elevations where no roads go. The scar on these hills will be there for a long time, until nature eventually brings back the area's beauty. The lessons from this wildfire include an understanding of how important safety is over beauty. Trees such as eucalyptus, which were imported from Australia to California in the 1800s, brought a volatile fuel to an overcrowded and poorly designed urban area.

It is very possible that the people of a city like Oakland hadn't considered the ramifications of an urban firestorm, even though they were surrounded by woods. A measure of balance is needed between the aesthetics of the area and the safety of those who live there. Oakland has taken this lesson to heart as a result of its loss and rebuilding process. Many planners have used other urban areas to plan for such an event; perhaps in doing so they can avoid the tragedy faced by the residents of Oakland.

CHAPTER 18
Shakedown in Los Angeles
NORTHRIDGE EARTHQUAKE
- 1994 -

THE SIMPLE FACTS OF THE NORTHRIDGE EARTHQUAKE are that at 4:31 on the morning of Monday, January 17, 1994, the San Fernando Valley of Los Angeles County was rattled by a magnitude 6.7 earthquake. It lasted fifteen seconds. It had an epicenter 9 miles deep under the town of Reseda, in the same general area as the Sylmar Earthquake of 1971, about 20 miles northwest of downtown Los Angeles. But the greatest damage occurred in the neighboring town of Northridge, hence the name of the quake.

A massive section of four-lane Interstate 5 collapsed in the 1994 Northridge earthquake. Governor's Office of Emergency Services

The death toll was 57, with 12,000 people injured. The total cost of recovery exceeded $40 billion, making this earthquake the most costly disaster in U.S. history to that time.

Los Angeles had been spared the grief and despair of the outcome of earthquakes for a long time. The Santa Barbara (1925) and the Long Beach (1933) temblors, like Sylmar, had been of moderate strength on the Richter scale's measurements. But Los Angeles County had no known major faults—the nearest was that of the San Andreas, which in Southern California runs down the central valley corridor, at its closest 60 miles from downtown. And while Northridge was also considered a moderate quake, it astonished scientists because it exposed the existence of hidden faults deep underground that had not been part of the geographical models being used at the time. Today, scientists believe that the unseen fault system under the L.A. metropolitan area may be so complex that it is potentially a greater—although up to now quieter—risk than the peril posed by the San Andreas Fault, which separates the California coast tectonic plate from the U.S. continental plate. And even with all the damage that was done in this earthquake—the most expensive natural disaster in U.S. history—there is that startling realization that this was not "The Big One."

Based on the knowledge gained from the 1971 Sylmar temblor, both the state of California and the city of Los Angeles made changes in construction codes for buildings and highways, strengthening the level and type of construction for earthquake safety purposes. The 1989 Loma Prieta quake in central and northern California showed that more changes were needed, and more efficient and safer designs were developed for the construction of roadways, especially bridges. A retrofit program for earthquake safety of highways and bridges in particular was established, and some of the work had already been done.

The first test of those changes came early on the morning of January 17, 1994. The city was again fortunate in the timing of the tremor—4:31 A.M.—and of the day, a holiday in observation of Dr. Martin Luther King Jr.'s birthday. Many who would ordinarily be rising to go to work or school instead had plans to sleep in. And while their plans were most definitely disrupted, their lives were most likely saved by these circumstances.

Movement of the quake showed tremendous acceleration—to nearly the force of gravity. The area of greatest damage was mostly within a 20-mile radius of the epicenter, including Santa Monica, on the coast.

Los Angeles depends on an intricate network of roads to move millions of people each day to and from work, school, and shopping. When one structure fails, the commute becomes longer as commuters move to local streets or smaller highways.

In this quake, however, no fewer than five major freeways were damaged to the point of closing. In a 6-mile stretch, the busiest freeway in the United States, the Santa Monica Freeway (I–10), buckled in three places. The interchange between the Golden State Freeway (I–5) and the Antelope Freeway (SR–14) collapsed, as it did in the 1971 quake. But the San Fernando Valley had grown, and hundreds of thousands more residents were affected. A ninety-minute commute became a six-hour nightmare for workers on Tuesday morning when businesses reopened.

While lives were spared by the early hour of the earthquake, the city and county were definitely not inured to its force. Apartment buildings with first-floor or basement carports collapsed, story falling upon story. At the Northridge Meadows Apartment building, according to one report, the survivors stated that the building first moved upward, then to the side, and finally down, hard, pancaking the floors and crushing fifteen people on the first floor.

Heroism was a going commodity that day, as people trapped in buildings were freed by passersby and emergency workers. In one instance a man helped an elderly woman out of the rubble and then went in himself to retrieve her purse. Thousands, however, were left homeless, and with the help of nonprofit agencies and the state, federal, and local governments, tents were brought in a day later to protect those without homes from the elements.

Only about one-quarter of homeowners and businesses affected by the earthquake had earthquake insurance, because the premiums for coverage in high-risk areas cost so much. One of the lessons homeowners throughout California learned from the Loma Prieta earthquake in 1989 was that if you think your house is going to be red-tagged by an inspector, get what you can out of the building before it happens. As in San Francisco, residents of homes that were marked for destruction were given up to fifteen minutes to retrieve items. Many went back in before the inspectors arrived to save precious items.

But many had had little when the quake hit, and now they had nothing. The poor, the new immigrants, and others living on the financial edge found themselves to be homeless, their buildings destroyed or soon to be demolished. While homeowners with earthquake insurance could rebuild, landlords—especially in areas where the poor lived—were not quick to replace the housing stock. Some replaced their original dilapidated holdings with units too expensive for the poor to rent. Others just didn't rebuild.

In Northridge Fashion Mall, the Bullocks Department Store collapsed from the shaking. While emergency workers found no one in the rubble, they did find hundreds of animals in the mall's pet store in need of attention.

California State University at Northridge suffered tremendous damage, causing the school to be closed. Again, luck was with would-be victims; the students were on winter break, about to return to college for spring semester the following Monday. And again lives were saved, but buildings were not. Portions of the roof of the Delmar T. Oviatt Library caved in; Sierra Tower, a seven-story building, was

A Los Angeles apartment complex. Governor's Office of Emergency Services

closed. The South Library building survived the initial quake, but aftershocks and an electrical fire caused significant damage. Science buildings 1 through 4 all suffered damage, with fire in building 2 and hazardous materials spilled in others. Finally, part of the four-story parking structure collapsed.

Vowing to start the spring semester within two weeks of its scheduled time, CSU-Northridge President Blenda Wilson set in motion the establishment of temporary quarters for classrooms and offices in portable buildings. The university leased 400 trailers to replace the more than one hundred buildings that had been damaged. It took several years to repair, retrofit, and rebuild the campus. Campus officials decided to demolish two wings of the Oviatt Library, the fine arts building, the South Library building, and an apartment building, along with the collapsed parking garage, rather than attempt to repair them.

The focus immediately after the quake was on loss of power throughout the county and on the safety of dams and reservoirs surrounding Los Angeles County. But public health officials warned early and often that water needed to be boiled before use. Damage to sewage and water lines were still being uncovered three years after the quake. And an oil spill on the Santa Clara River in northern Los Angeles County (near the site of the destroyed St. Francis Dam) dumped 3,500 gallons into the water and onto the river's banks.

The surprise of the earthquake was found out months after the damage was first estimated. Cursory observations of high-rise steel buildings showed them to be safe, but when more closely inspected, these buildings were found to be in disrepair.

Many lessons were learned from the quake. Building and highway construction codes were again changed and strengthened. Scientists learned that their belief that Los Angeles had no major faults was false. More people learned earthquake preparedness. And most of all, Angelenos learned that, at any moment and without warning, life can be disrupted and lost. As the area continues to grow, more people ignore the dangers of living in quake-prone areas so that they can enjoy the California sun, gambling that what happened that day in January, 1994, will not happen in their lifetimes. All the while, they know that the big one, predicted to destroy them, is but a moment away.

CHAPTER 19

For the Loss of a Screw

CRASH OF ALASKA AIRLINES 261
- 2000 -

A TYPICAL DAY IN THE LIFE OF A COMMERCIAL aircraft starts the night before. The plane goes through a preflight checkup—partly a visual inspection and partly an inspection based on the plane's mileage. Maintenance procedures are set and approved by the FAA. The rules are followed, because there are just too many

This jackscrew assembly's failure caused the demise of Alaska Airlines 261. NTSB

lives at risk in a vital part's failure. The passengers depend on the pilot to get them there. The pilot depends on the mechanics to get them there safely.

The last day of this Alaska Airlines MD-83, a low wing, two-engine jet, started as usual at about 2:00 A.M. on February 1, 2000, in snowy Anchorage, Alaska, on the first leg of its journey to its eventual destination, Puerto Vallarta, Mexico. It would stop in Seattle, Washington, and San Francisco. In Puerto Vallarta it would turn around and with a new crew return to Seattle via San Francisco.

The southbound flight, known as Flight 158, was uneventful. The snow turned to rain in Seattle, then to showers in San Francisco. But Puerto Vallarta was beautifully warm and sunny at 12:30 in the afternoon. The plane, however, did not linger, and by 1:35 P.M., it was back in the air as Flight 261, on its way to San Francisco.

The plane headed toward 31,000 feet above sea level, its cruising altitude. Traveling at 330 knots on autopilot, at 28,000 feet the autopilot was turned off, and according to the data control recorder, the plane was flown manually for the next two hours. During this time a force of as much as fifty pounds was used on the control columns, an unusually strong force. The crew contacted Alaska Airlines maintenance in Seattle directly during this time to try to diagnose and fix the horizontal stabilizer that was jammed.

At 3:47 P.M., the autopilot was reengaged. Two minutes later, the captain contacted the Mazatlan control center for permission to divert to Los Angeles International Airport (LAX) from its planned route to San Francisco. After some negotiations as to whether it would be better to land in San Francisco or LAX, including weather conditions and which runways were being used, Alaska Airlines Dispatch in Seattle agreed to the pilot's request not to bypass an available airport capable of handling a jet the size of the MD-83. The decision was made to bring the aircraft to Los Angeles.

Since Flight 261 was coming from Puerto Vallarta, it was an international flight, and a change of destinations required the gaining of landing rights from the Immigration and Naturalization Service. Traffic control was handed off to the LAX air controller. The plane was about 90 miles from the Los Angeles terminal.

At 4:08 P.M., a mechanic in Alaska's maintenance facility in LAX asked, "Did you try the suitcase handles and the pickle switches?" colloquial references to various trim switches that the pilot can access. "Yeah," replied the captain. "We tried everything together." And they affirmed that they had tried the alternate trim systems, but everything seemed either jammed or not working.

The pilot decided to test the horizontal stabilizer again. At 4:09:16, the autopilot was disengaged. Three seconds later, the sound of a "clunk" was heard on the cockpit voice recorder (CVR), and the stabilizer moved to a 2.5-degree nose-down position. For the next eighty seconds, the plane dived, gaining speed to 353 knots and dropping about 8,000 feet.

4:09:26	Captain:	"It got worse."
4:09:52	Captain to first officer:	"Help me back, help me back."
4:09:54	First officer:	"OK."
4:09:55	Captain to control tower:	"Center Alaska two sixty one, we are in a dive here."
4:10:01	Captain to control tower:	"I've lost control, vertical pitch."
4:10:01	(sound of the overspeed warning, which continued for the next thirty-three seconds)	
4:10:05	Controller:	"Alaska two sixty one say again sir."
4:10:06	Captain to control tower:	"Yeah, we're out of twenty-six thousand feet, we are in a vertical dive . . . not a dive yet . . . but uh we've lost vertical control of our airplane."
4:10:20	Captain:	"Just help me."

4:10:22   Captain: "Once we get the speed slowed maybe . . . we'll be OK."

4:10:28   Captain to control tower: "We're at twenty-three seven, request uh. . . ."

4:10:33   Captain to control tower: "Yeah, we got it back under control here."

4:10:34   First officer: "No, we don't."

In the cockpit tensions increased between the pilot and the first officer:

4:10:45   First officer: "Let's take the speed brakes off . . ."

4:10:46   Captain: "No, no leave them there. It seems to be helping."

4:10:55   Captain: "OK, it really wants to pitch down."

4:10:58   First officer: "OK."

4:10:59   Captain: "Don't mess with that."

4:11:04   First officer: "I agree with you."

At 4:11:06.6, the captain announced to air traffic control that the plane was "kinda stabilized" at about 24,000 feet. "We're slowing here, and uh, we're gonna uh, do a little troubleshooting, can you gimme a block between uh, twenty and twenty-five?"

"Alaska two sixty one maintain block altitude flight level two zero zero through flight level two five zero," a controller responded.

The test of the suitcase handles and pickle switches had failed. The crew realized that they were even worse off than before because the stabilizer was now in a worse jam, and they were fighting to keep the plane at altitude. They were out over the water, but they were running too fast. The plane was fighting them for stability.

At 4:14:12 the captain got on the intercom and spoke to the passengers: "Folks, we have had a flight control problem up front here we're workin' it; uh, that's Los Angeles off to the right there, that's where we're intending to go. We're pretty busy up here workin' this situation. I don't anticipate any big problems once we get a couple of subsystems on the line. But we will be going into LAX, and I'd anticipate us parking there in about twenty to thirty minutes."

Switched off to the next controller at 20 miles from the airport, the captain wanted to test the plane's feel at lower speeds by bringing it down to 10,000 feet. The controller wanted them to come down to 17,000 feet. They dropped the slats and flaps 11 degrees as they slowed the plane to 250 knots; the captain told the first officer that the plane felt pretty stable, but he wanted to get down to 180 knots. They brought up the flaps and slats.

4:18:37　Captain: "What I want to do . . . is get the nose up . . . and then let the nose fall through and see if we can stab it when it's unloaded."

4:18:56　First officer: "Do you mean use this again? I don't think we should. If it can fly, it's like . . . "

4:19:01　Captain: "It's on the stop now, it's on the stop."

4:19:04　First officer: "Well, not according to that, it's not."

4:19:07　First officer: "The trim might be, and then it might be, uh, if something's popped back there . . . "

4:19:11　First officer: "It might be . . . mechanical damage, too."

4:19:14　Captain: "I think if it's controllable, we oughta just try to land it . . . "

4:19:16　Captain: "You think so? OK, let's head for LA."

4:19:21　(sound of a thump)

4:19:24　First officer: "You feel that?"
　　　　　Captain: "Yeah."

The recorder picked up the sound of clicks from movement of slat/flap handle, as well as a loud voice. The sound of loose articles hitting hard objects increased.

4:19:43 First officer: "Mayday!"

4:19:49 Captain: "Push and roll, push and roll."

4:19:54 Captain: "OK, we're inverted . . . and now we gotta get it . . ."

4:20:03 Captain: "Kick [expletive] push, push, push . . . push the blue side up. Push."

4:20:14 First officer: "I'm pushing."

4:20:16 Captain: "OK, now let's kick rudder . . . left rudder, left rudder."

First officer: "I can't reach it."

Captain: "Okay, right rudder . . . right rudder."

4:20:25 Captain: "Are we flyin? . . . we're flyin . . . we're flyin . . . tell 'em what we're doin'."

4:20:38 Captain: "Gotta get it over again . . . at least upside down we're flyin'."

4:20:54 Captain: "Speed brakes."

4:20:55 First officer: "Got it."

4:20:56 Captain: "Ah, here we go."

4:20:57 (recording ends)

Drew Gottshall, a maintenance worker for the National Park Service, worked on Anacapa, a small island in Channel Islands National Park, off the coast southeast of Point Hueneme. It is a quiet place, and the sound of a plane low overhead caught Gottshall's attention. Turning his head toward the ocean, he watched as a large plane fell out of the sky, corkscrewing into the sea. According to newspaper articles, here's what Gottshall witnessed: "The plane made a quick entry into the water upon impact and disappeared. It had a finality to it that came very quickly."

Several pilots in the vicinity also watched the plane's dramatic dive. All eighty-eight people on board died. Impact tore the plane apart; the plane's wreckage was carried by the strong currents. The

Coast Guard began a search and rescue in the cold, choppy waters.

Squid fishermen in the area joined the Coast Guard in collecting whatever pieces of the plane they found, but only the official search party handled the bodies spotted by the irregulars. By nightfall only one body had been found.

The ocean floor in the area was as deep as 700 feet, making recovery that much more difficult. The Coast Guard called on the National Ocean Service and the National Oceanic and Atmospheric Association for help in mapping the area and other assistance. Using the Hazardous Materials Assessment Division's (HAZMAT) oil-spill projection program, the Coast Guard was able to project how the debris would move and disperse.

Since scuba divers cannot go below 300 feet, the navy brought in the supervisor of salvage from the Naval Sea Systems Command. Its submarine rescue support ship, operated by the navy's Deep Submergence Unit, was sent to the site. Using the Remotely Operated Vehicle (ROV) Scorpio, the aircraft's black boxes were found and retrieved.

Recovery of the bodies started on February 4. Deep Drone, another navy ROV, was used to bring them to the surface. On February 10, Deep Drone recovered the tail section of the plane and its horizontal stabilizer, the key to understanding the cause of this tremendous loss.

The National Transportation Safety Board investigated for nearly three years. On December 30, 2002, in its final report, it found:

- The longitudinal trim control system was functioning normally until it jammed as the plane reached 23,400 feet on its assent from Puerto Vallarta International Airport; the plane continued to rise to 31,000 feet with the stabilizer in this position.
- The longitudinal trim control system failed because of the shearing of the worn threads of the horizontal stabilizer acme nut by the acme screw.

- The jam was caused by the lack of lubrication of the acme screw.
- The first dive was caused when the jam was overcome as the crew attempted to use the trim motor. When released, the acme screw pulled up through its nut, which forced the horizontal stabilizer into an upward position; this position forces the plane to pitch downward.
- The acme nut and screw did not completely separate because the screw's lower mechanical stop was restrained by the lower surface of the acme nut; the pilot was then able to regain control of the aircraft.
- The broken jackscrew assembly (acme screw and nut) gave way a second before the final dive because of the fatigue fracture of the torque tube, which then brought about the failure of the vertical stabilizer tip fairing brackets, so that the horizontal stabilizer could then pitch farther forward than it was designed to do.
- The jackscrew assembly failed because there was no lubrication of the acme screw and nut, due to the extended lubrication intervals Alaska used.

Alaska Airlines had asked the Federal Aviation Administration for permission to extend its lubrication intervals on the MD-83s in its fleet. The FAA had granted permission based on the recommendation of Boeing, which had bought McDonnell Douglas in 1996. It was during this extended period between lubrications that the assembly had lost lubrication, which caused the screw to shear off the nut's threads. Had the intervals been of normal duration, the assembly, which was wearing excessively, would have been inspected and replaced or repaired as needed. The NTSB further stated that there was no technical data produced to support Alaska's request for these extensions as safe. "The absence of a fail-safe mechanism to prevent the catastrophic effects of total acme nut thread loss contributed to the Alaska Airlines flight 261 accident."

Bibliography

Lost in the Frozen Sierra: Donner Party (1846–1847)

DeLafosse, Peter, ed. *Trailing the Pioneers: A Guide to Utah's Emigrant Trails, 1829–1869*. Logan, Utah: Utah State University Press, 1994.

Gibbons, Bond. "The Itch to Move West." *National Geographic*, Vol. 170, No. 2, August 1986.

Hastings, Lansford. *The Emigrant's Guide to Oregon and California in 1845*.

Houghton, Eliza P. Donner. *The Expedition of the Donner Party and Its Tragic Fate*. Lincoln: University of Nebraska Press, 1997.

McGlashan, C. F. *History of the Donner Party: A Tragedy of the Sierra, 1881*, Palo Alto, Calif: Stanford University Press, 1940.

Ship-Killing Rocks: Wrecks Off Point Honda (1854 and 1923)

Harrison, Tim and Ray Jones. *Lost Lighthouses*. Guilford, Conn.: Globe Pequot Press, 2000.

Knight, Donald and Eugene Wheeler. *Agony and Death on a Gold Rush Steamer: The Disastrous Sinking of the Side-Wheeler* Yankee Blade. Oxnard: Pathfinder Publications of California, 1990.

The Colorado Changes Course: Making of the Salton Sea (1905)

Carle, David. *Introduction to Water in California*. Berkeley: University of California Press, 2004.

Cleeland, Nancy. "Out of One-Time Disaster, a Fishing Oasis Was Born," *San Diego Union Tribune*, February 1, 1983.

DeBuys, William Eno. *Salt Dreams: Land and Water in Low-Down California*. Albuquerque: University of New Mexico Press, 1999.

James, George Wharton. *The Wonders of the Colorado Desert (Southern California); Its Rivers and Its Mountains, Its Canyons and Its Springs, Its Life and Its History, Pictured and Described; Including an Account of a Recent Journey Made Down the Overflow of the Colorado River to the Mysterious Salton Sea.* Boston: Little, Brown, and Company, 1906.

"The Salton Sea," a Web site maintained by the San Diego State University Center for Inland Waters: www.sci.sdsu.edu/salton/SaltonSeaHomePage.html.

Terror in San Francisco: Earthquake and Fire (1906)

Fradkin, Philip L. *The Great Earthquake and Firestorms of 1906: How San Francisco Nearly Destroyed Itself.* Berkeley: University of California Press, 2005.

Hansen, Gladys and Emmet Condon. *Denial of Disaster: The Untold Story and Photographs of the San Francisco Earthquake and Fire of 1906.* San Francisco: Cameron and Company, 1989.

Kurzman, Dan. *Disaster! The Great San Francisco Earthquake and Fire of 1906.* New York: William Morrow, 2001.

London, Jack. "The Story of an Eyewitness." Originally published in *Collier's*, May 5, 1906. Retrieved from the Berkeley Digital Library SunSite Web site: sunsite.berkeley.edu/London/Writings/Journalism/sfearthquake.html.

Morris, Charles, ed. *The San Francisco Calamity by Earthquake and Fire.* Urbana: University of Illinois Press, 2002.

Saul, Eric and Don Denevi. *The Great San Francisco Earthquake and Fire, 1906.* Millbrae, Calif.: Celestial Arts, 1981.

Turner, Patricia, ed. *1906 Remembered: Firsthand Accounts of the San Francisco Disaster.* San Francisco: Friends of the San Francisco Public Library, 1981.

Virtual Museum of the City of San Francisco Web site: "Earthquake Newspaper Clippings." www.sfmuseum.org/press/clip.html.

———"Eyewitness Accounts." www.sfmuseum.org/1906/ew.html.

———"Mayor Eugene Schmitz' Famed 'Shoot To Kill' order—April 18, 1906." www.sfmuseum.org/1906.2/killproc.html.

———"1906 Earthquake Relief and Recovery Efforts." www.sfmuseum.org/1906/recovery.html.

——— "Police Department Report." www.sfmuseum.org/1906/06pd1.html.
——— "San Francisco Fire Department History of the Great Earthquake and Fire." www.sfmuseum.org/1906/sffd.html.
——— "San Francisco One Year Later." www.sfmuseum.org/hist11/sfoneyearlater.html.
——— "Southern Pacific and the 1906 Earthquake." www.sfmuseum.org/1906/spco.html.
——— "U.S. Army Operations during the Great Earthquake and Fire." www.sfmuseum.org/1906/armyops.html.
——— "U.S. Navy Operations during the Great Earthquake and Fire." www.sfmuseum.org/1906/navops.html.

Crime of the Century: Los Angeles Times Bombing (1910)

Adamic, Louis. *Dynamite: The Story of Class Violence in America*. New York: The Viking Press, 1934.

"The Bombing of the Los Angeles Times." Los Angeles Fire Department Historical Archive, on the L.A. Fire Web site: www.lafire.com/famous_fires/100110_LATimesFire/100110_TimesFire.htm.

Cowan, Geoffrey. *The People v. Clarence Darrow: The Bribery Trial of America's Greatest Lawyer*. New York: Times Books, 1993.

Faulkner, Harold U. "The Rise of the Labor Movement in Los Angeles." *The Journal of Economic History*, Vol. 16, No. 2, June 1956, pp. 260–61.

Foner, Philip S. *"A Martyr to His Cause*: The Scenario of the First Labor Film in the United States." *Labor History*, Vol. 24, No. 1, 1983, pp. 103–11.

Johnson, Daniel J. "'No Make-Believe Class Struggle': The Socialist Municipal Campaign in Los Angeles, 1911." *Labor History*, Vol. 41, No. 1, 2000, pp. 25–46.

Nadeau, Remi. *Los Angeles: From Mission to Modern City*. New York: Longmans, Green, 1960.

Fire in the Hole:
Argonaut Mine Disaster (1922)

"Jackson." *Sierra Foothill Magazine* Web site: www.sierrafoothillmagazine.com/jackson.html.

Mace, O. Henry. *47 Down: The 1922 Argonaut Gold Mine Disaster*. New York: John Wiley and Sons, 2004.

Pickard, Byron O. *Lessons from the Fire in the Argonaut Mine*. Washington, D.C.: United States Government Printing Office, 1926.

Mulholland's Dam Falls:
St. Francis Reservoir Flood (1928)

McWilliams, Carey. *Southern California: An Island on the Land*. Salt Lake City: Gibbs Smith, 1973.

Nunis, Doyce Blackman and Charles N. Johnson. *The St. Francis Dam Disaster Revisited*. Los Angeles: Historical Society of Southern California, 1995.

Outland, Charles. *Man-Made Disaster: The Story of St. Francis Dam*. Glendale, Calif.: Arthur H. Clark Company, 1963.

"The San Francisquito Canyon and the St. Francis Dam." Santa Clarita Valley History in Pictures on the Santa Clarita Valley Historical Society Web site: www.scvhistory.com/scvhistory/stfrancis.htm.

Friendly Fire:
Port Chicago Explosion (1944)

Allen, Robert L. *The Port Chicago Mutiny*. New York: Warner Books, 1989.

Bell, Christopher L. and Bruce A. Elleman. *Naval Mutinies of the Twentieth Century: An International Perspective*. London: Frank Cass, 2003.

The San Fernando Earthquake of 1971: A Preliminary Report Published Jointly by the U.S. Geological Survey and the National Oceanic and Atmospheric Administration. Washington, D.C.: United States Government Printing Office, 1971.

Trapped by Flame:
Rattlesnake Forest Fire (1953)

Maclean, John N. *Fire and Ashes: On the Front Lines of American Wildfire*. New York: Henry Holt and Company, 2003.

"Staff Ride to the Rattlesnake Fire," Wildland Fire Leadership Development Program Web site: www.fireleadership.gov/toolbox/staffride/library_staff_ride2.html.

Rains That Wouldn't Stop:
Santa Cruz Christmas Flood (1955)

"The 1950s: The Great Flood of '55." *Santa Cruz Sentinel* Online Edition: www.santacruzsentinel.com/extra/century/52/.

Staff of Flood Control Function of the Division of Water Resources of the State of California. *Floods of December 1955 in California*. Sacramento, Calif.: Division of Water Resources, 1956.

Wall of Water:
Crescent City Tsunami (1964)

"Crescent City Remembers 1964 Tsunami." *San Francisco Chronicle*, SFGate.com Web site: www.sfgate.com/cgi-bin/article.cgi?f=/news/archive/2005/01/01/state2002EST0057.DTL.

"Crescent City's 1964 Tsunami." *Jackson County* (Oregon) *Mail Tribune Online*: www.mailtribune.com/archive/2005/0203/local/stories/01local.htm.

Davidson, Keay. "Ancient Sands Reveal Traces of Huge Tsunamis: Layers in Soil Cores Could Help Predict Future Disasters." *San Francisco Chronicle*, at SFGate Web site: www.sfgate.com/cgibin/article.cgi?f=/c/a/2005/06/13/MNG8HD7O0V1.DTL&hw=tsunami+crescent+city&sn=001&sc=1000.

"Death and Disaster along the Humboldt Coast." National Park Service Web site: www.cr.nps.gov/history/online_books/redw/history12b.htm.

Drye, Willie. "California Tsunami Victims Recall 1964's Killer Waves." *National Geographic News,* January 21, 2005. Retrieved from National Geographic News Web site: news.nationalgeographic.com/news/2005/01/0121_050121_1964_tsunami.html.

"March 28, 1964 Alaska Tsunami." West Coast and Alaska Tsunami Warning Center (NOAA) Web site: wcatwc.arh.noaa.gov/web_tsus/19640328/narrative8.htm.

Pararas-Carayannis, George. "The Effects of the March 27, 1964, Alaska Tsunami in California." From The Tsunami Page Web site: www.drgeorgepc.com/Tsunami1964Calif.html.

Powers, Dennis M. *The Raging Sea*. New York: Citadel Press, 2005.

"Tsunami!" The Redwood Coast Tsunami Work Group Web site: www.humboldt.edu/~geodept/earthquakes/tsunami!/Tsunami!_TOC.html.

"Tsunami Once Killed in California." ABC News Web site: http://abcnews.go.com/WNT/Tsunami/story?id=398217&page=1.

"Tsunamis." Washington State Department of Natural Resources Web site: www.dnr.wa.gov/geology/hazards/tsunami.htm.

He Shot the Pilot:
Crashes of PAL 773 and PSA 1771 (1964 and 1987)

Notable California Aviation Disasters Web site: "California's 10 Worst Crashes." http://members.aol.com/jaydeebee1/aviation.html.

——— "The 1950s." http://members.aol.com/jaydeebee1/crash50s.html.

——— "The 1980s." http://members.aol.com/jaydeebee1/crash80s.html.

The Longest Minute:
Sylmar Earthquake (1971)

California Geology San Fernando Earthquake Edition, No. 24, 4–5, April/May 1971. Retrieved from the Los Angeles Fire Department Historical Archive Web site: http://lafire.com/famous_fires/710209_Sylmar Earthquake/1971-0500_SF-EqEdition_1971SFEarthquake.htm:

——— Douglas, M. "Seismically Triggered Landslides above San Fernando Valley."

——— Greensfelder, Roger. "Seismologic and Crustal Movement Investigations of the San Fernando Earthquake."
——— Kahle, J. E. et al. "Geologic Surface Effects of the San Fernando Earthquake."
——— "The 1971 Sylmar Earthquake."
——— Oakeshott, Gordon B. "The Geologic Setting."
——— "San Andreas Blamed for San Fernando Quake."
——— Saul, R. R. "Effects of the San Fernando Earthquake in the Oat Mountain Quadrangle."
"Killer Quake." *Los Angeles Herald Examiner Extra,* Vol. 318, February 9, 1971, p. 1. Retrieved from the Los Angeles Fire Department Historical Archive: http://lafire.com/famous_fires/710209_ SylmarEarthquake/020971_LAHerald_KillerQuake.htm.

We've Been Hit:
Major Airline Collisions (1971, 1978, and 1986)

"Aircraft Accident Report, Pacific Southwest Airlines, Inc., B-727, N533PS, and Gibbs Flite Center, Inc., Cessna-172, N7711G, San Diego, California, September 25, 1978." National Transportation Safety Board, April 20, 1979.
"CVR Transcript PSA Boeing 727." Direct Net @ccess Users Web site: http://dnausers.d-n-a.net/dnetGOjg/250978.htm.
"Eyewitness Report: PSA 182." AirDisaster.com Web site: www.airdisaster.com/eyewitness/psa182.shtml.
Notable California Aviation Disasters Web site: "California's 10 Worst Crashes." http://members.aol.com/jaydeebee1/aviation.html.
——— "The 1970s." http://members.aol.com/jaydeebee1/crash70s.html.
——— "The 1980s." http://members.aol.com/jaydeebee1/crash80s.html.
"The PSA history page," PSA Oldtimes page from Cactuswings.com Web site: www.cactuswings.com/psa/museum/crash.htm.

World Series Earthquake: Loma Prieta (1989)

Santa Cruz Sentinel, Loma Prieta Earthquake Anniversary Edition, Sunday, October 17, 1999. Holbrook, Stet. "The Cost in Dollars and Cents." www.santacruzsentinel.com/special/specquake/quake9.htm.
——— Lydon, Sandy. "Return to the Epicenter." www.santacruzsentinel.com/special/specquake/quake5.htm.
——— Musitelli, Robin. "Quake Triggered 1,000 Landslides in SC." www.santacruzsentinel.com/special/specquake/quake11.htm.
——— Pittman, Jennifer. "A Downtown Transformed." www.santacruzsentinel.com/special/specquake/quake3.htm.
——— "Ten Years After." www.santacruzsentinel.com/special/specquake/quake1.htm.
——— White, Dan. "Haphazard Chance Chose the Victims, the Rescuers." www.santacruzsentinel.com/special/specquake/quake6.htm.
——— Wong, May. "County Smoothes the Wrinkles Out of Disaster Response Plan." www.santacruzsentinel.com/special/specquake/quake4.htm.
Virtual Museum of the City of San Francisco Web site: Fowler, Dave. "The Initial Response to the Cypress Freeway Disaster." www.sfmuseum.net/cypress/response.html.
——— "San Francisco Earthquake History 1915–1989." www.sfmuseum.org/alm/quakes3.html.
"Where Can I Learn More about the 1989 Earthquake?" University of California Berkeley Seismology Laboratory Web site: http://seismo.berkeley.edu/seismo/faq/1989_0.html.
Wilson, Richard C. *The Loma Prieta Quake: What One City Learned.* Washington, D.C.: International City Management Association, 1991.

Poisoning the Sacramento: Dunsmuir Toxic Spill (1991)

"Cantara Loop/Dunsmuir Chemical Spill." Department of Fish and Game, Office of Spill Prevention and Response Web site: www.dfg.ca.gov/ospr/organizational/scientific/nrda/NRDAcantara.htm.

Garvin, Cosmo. "Injunction Junction." *Sacramento News and Review,* October 16, 2003. Retrieved from the *Sacramento News and Review* Web site: www.newsreview.com/issues/sacto/2003-10-16/news3.asp.

Kreutzer, R. "Acute Health Effects of the Cantara Metam-Sodium Spill: An Epidemiologic Assessment." Environmental Health Investigations Branch, California Department of Health Services, 1992. Retrieved from the EHIB Web site: www.ehib.org/cma/papers/22_Kreutzer_1992_Acute.pdf.

Martin, Jim. "The Dead River: A Visit to the 1991 Dunsmuir Toxic Spill," parts 1 and 2. Orgone Biophysical Research Laboratory Web site: www.orgonelab.org/DeadRiv1.htm and www.orgonelab.org/DeadRiv2.htm.

Smith, Matt. "Is This Any Way to Run a Railroad?" *SF Weekly,* August 12, 1998. Retrieved from *SF Weekly* Web site: www.sfweekly.com/issues/1998-08-12/news/feature2_print.html.

"Spill Kills Summer on the Sacramento." *Los Angeles Times,* July 19, 1991. Retrieved from Kevin Roderick.com Web site: www.kevinroderick.com/spill.html.

"10 Years after the Southern Pacific Railroad Spill the Upper Sacramento River is Re-born: An Update by *California Trout,*" July 13, 2001. *California Trout* Web site: www.caltrout.org/comm/pressreleases/UpperSacJuly01.htm.

"A Toxic Nightmare: The Dunsmuir Metam Sodium Spill Revisited." *Sonoma County Free Press* Web site: www.sonomacountyfreepress.com/reaction/a_toxic_nightmare.html.

Voyage, Richard C. "How Much Is a River Worth?: Assessing Damage in the Dunsmuir Spill." *California Lawyer,* Vol. 14, No. 8, August 1994, pp. 31–37.

Burning Hills: Oakland Tunnel Fire (1991)

"Abstract." National Wildland/Urban Interface Program's Firewise Web site: www.firewise.org/pubs/theOaklandBerkeleyHillsFire/.

Bredeson, Carmen. *Fire in Oakland, California: Billion-Dollar Blaze.* Berkeley Heights, N.J.: Enslow Publishers, 1999.

"California Burning." *People Weekly,* Vol. 36, No. 17, November 4, 1991, p. 44.

O'Lone, Richard G. and Breck W. Henderson. "Airborne Imaging, GPS Aid Aircraft." *Aviation Week and Space Technology,* Vol. 135, No. 17, October 28, 1991, p. 70.

"'Two Days of Hell' in Alameda County, CA." Emergency Response and Research Institute Web site: www.emergency.com/firepage.htm.

Virtual Museum of the City of San Francisco Web site: "Extract from the Minutes of the San Francisco Fire Commission, Tuesday, October 22, 1991." www.sfmuseum.org/oakfire/minutes.html.

—— "San Francisco Fire Department, Central Fire Alarm Station." www.sfmuseum.org/oakfire/cfas.html.

—— Parker, Captain Donald R. "The Oakland-Berkeley Hills Fire: An Overview."

Shakedown in Los Angeles: Northridge Earthquake (1994)

Bolin, Robert, with Lois Stanford. *The Northridge Earthquake: Vulnerability and Disaster.* London: Routledge, 1998.

Holzer, Thomas L. "Predicting Earthquake Effects: Learning from Northridge and Loma Prieta." *Science,* Vol. 265, August 26, 1994, pp. 1182–83.

"The January 17, 1994 Northridge, CA Earthquake: An EQE Summary Report. March 1994." Los Angeles Fire Department Historical Archive Web site: http://lafire.com/famous_fires/940117_NorthridgeEarthquake/quake/00_EQE_contents.htm.

Proquest Newsstand database: "An End and a Beginning." *Los Angeles Times* editorial, March 7, 1999, p. 16.

—— Enriquez, Sam. "Earthquake: The Long Road Back: CSUN President Hopes to Reopen Campus Feb. 7." *Los Angeles Times,* January 20, 1994, p. 8.

—— Haynes, Karinma A. "Los Angeles; The Northridge Earthquake: 10 Years Later," *Los Angeles Times,* January 16, 2004, p. B3.

—— Hotz, Robert Lee. "Amid Ruins, Clues to Deep Mysteries." *Los Angeles Times,* January 19, 1994, p. 1.

——"Jan. 17, 1994, Is Still with Us." *Los Angeles Times* editorial, January 17, 1997, p. 8.

——Johnson, Reed. "The Northridge Earthquake: 10 Years Later," *Los Angeles Times*, January 17, 2004, p. E1.

——Kaplan, Sam. "Perspectives on the Northridge Earthquake." *Los Angeles Times,* January 18, 1994, p. 7.

——Martin, Hugo. "'94 Quake Damage to Sewer Lines Still Found." *Los Angeles Times*, August 11, 1997, p. 1.

——Moore, Solomon. "Back to Normal; Quake Aftermath: CSUN Students Voice Appreciation for New Buildings as the Last Portables Are Removed from the East Side of Campus." *Los Angeles Times,* November 22, 1997, p.1.

——Pearson, Erik et al. "Night of Terror: Awaking to the End of the World." *Orange County Register,* January 18, 1994, p. A04.

——Pool, Bob. "Los Angeles; The Northridge Earthquake: 10 Years Later." *Los Angeles Times*, January 16, 2004, p. B3.

——"Quake Death Toll Rises." *Orlando* (FL) *Sentinel,* January 20, 1994, p. A-1.

——"Shared Memories; The Northridge Earthquake: Five Years Later; Letters of Life, Death and Love." *Los Angeles Times*, January 17, 1999, p. 6.

——Somini-Sengupta, Curtis L. "Dazed and Aftershocked Highway Chaos; Clinton Sees Ruin." *New York Newsday*, January 20, 1994.

——Stassel, Stephanie. "Disaster Strikes Again and Again in the Valley." *Los Angeles Times*, December 14, 1999, p. 1.

——Waldie, D. J. "The Northridge Earthquake: 10 Years Later; Commentary." *Los Angeles Times,* January 17, 2004, p. E1.

——Weinstein, Henry. "Legal Aftershocks Will Keep Lots of Lawyers Busy." *Los Angeles Times,* January 30, 1994.

——Wilson, Tracy. "The Long Road Back; Massive Relief Effort Puts Red Cross Teams to the Test." *Los Angeles Times,* January 20, 1994, p. 3.

——"With Freeways Damaged, Angelenos Face Commuting 'Nightmare.'" *Chicago Tribune*, January 18, 1994, p. 11.

For the Loss of a Screw: Crash of Alaska Airlines 261 (2000)

Adair, Bill. "Inquiry Centers on Doomed Jet's Tail; Series: Alaska Airlines Flight 261." *St. Petersburg Times,* February 2, 2000, p. 1A.

"Aircraft Accident Report: Loss of Control and Impact with Pacific Ocean, Alaska Airlines Flight 261, McDonnell Douglas MD 83 N963AS, about 2.7 miles North of Anacapa Island, California, January 31, 2000." National Transportation Safety Board, adopted December 30, 2002, from NTSB Web site: www.ntsb.gov/publictn/2002/AAR0201.pdf.

"Alaska Admits Blame for California Crash." *Airwise News,* June 4, 2003, Web site: http://news.airwise.com/stories/2003/06/1054725051.html.

"Alaska Airlines Works Hard to Keep Its Good Reputation." *Oregonian,* February 6, 2000, p. B01.

Bailey, Brendan et al. "S.F.-Bound Jet Down." *San Jose Mercury-News,* February 1, 2000, p. 1A.

Cabanatuan, Michael et al. "Jet's Tail, 2nd Data Box Found; Recorder Reveals Pilots' Struggle with Stabilizer." *San Francisco Chronicle,* February 4, 2000, p. A1.

Garcia, Edward et al. "Chilling Accounts of Crash 'Corkscrewing': Nearby Pilots Describe Plunge." *San Jose Mercury-News,* February 3, 2000, p. 1A.

Hubert, Cynthia et al. "6-Minute Struggle in Midair, Ill-Fated Jet Crew Fought to Repair Balky Stabilizer." *Sacramento Bee,* February 2, 2000, p. A1.

Mecoy, Laura. "Some Families Moved to Tears by Grim Details; Medical Examiner Holds Briefing." *Sacramento Bee,* February 3, 2000, p. A12.

Taylor, Michael et al. "Jet's Frantic Final Minutes: Pilot Fought to Control Plane—Black Box Detected in Sea." *San Francisco Chronicle,* February 2, 2000, p. A1.

Weigand, Steve. "Descent into an Ocean of Sadness: When a Plane Crashes, the Effects Spread, Like Ripples on the Water, Touching the Lives of Everyone." *Sacramento Bee,* February 6, 2000, p. A1.

"California's 10 Worst Crashes." Notable California Aviation Disasters Web site: http://members.aol.com/jaydeebee1/aviation.html.

Manning, Jeff and Jennifer Bjorhus. "A Rough Course in the Wake of the Crash of Flight 251."

Murray, Michael. "Alaska Air Crash Story." Rain Public Interest Internet Web site: www.rain.org/pipermail/cinms-advisory-l/2001-March/000191.html.

About the Authors

Ray Jones is a publishing consultant and marketing specialist living in Pebble Beach, California. He is the author or coauthor of more than thirty books on American culture, natural history, architecture, and lighthouses, including both the award-winning *Lighthouse Encyclopedia* and *Legendary Lighthouses,* the best-selling companion to the PBS series of the same name.

Joe Lubow, formerly Merrill College Librarian and Fellow at the University of California at Santa Cruz, has worked as an editor and author for more than twenty years. He has co-written two books on California living and travel. His books with the Globe Pequot Press include *Choose a College Town for Retirement*. After many years away from academia, he recently returned to work at the California State University Monterey Bay Library. He lives in Marina, California.

THE INSIDER'S SOURCE

With more than 540 West-related titles, we have the area covered. Whether you're looking for the path less traveled, a favorite place to eat, family-friendly fun, a breathtaking hike, or enchanting local attractions, our pages are filled with ideas to get you from one state to the next.

For a complete listing of all our titles, please visit our Web site at www.GlobePequot.com. The Globe Pequot Press is the largest publisher of local travel books in the United States and is a leading source for outdoor recreation guides.

FOR BOOKS TO THE WEST

INSIDERS' GUIDE®
FALCON GUIDE®

Available wherever books are sold.
Orders can also be placed on the Web at www.GlobePequot.com, by phone from 8:00 A.M. to 5:00 P.M. at 1-800-243-0495, or by fax at 1-800-820-2329.